Upon This Rock

John Henry

Upon This Rock

Copyright © 2025 by John Henry

All rights reserved.

No part of this publication may be reproduced, stored in a retrieval system, or transmitted in any form or by any means—electronic, mechanical, photocopying, recording, or otherwise—without the prior written permission of the publisher, except for brief quotations used in reviews, articles, or scholarly reference with proper citation.

Published by: Always Toward the Light

www.AlwaysTowardTheLight.org

Cover Image:

Jesus Gives the Keys to Saint Peter by Luis Santos. Used with permission under standard license from Adobe Stock.

All Scripture passages are taken from the *Revised Standard Version Catholic Edition (RSVCE)*, © Division of Christian Education of the National Council of the Churches of Christ in the United States of America.

Scripture references may have light editorial adjustments made for clarity and readability in context.

Softcover Print Edition ISBN: 979-8-9996655-0-8

Genre: Religion / Spirituality

First Edition: 2025

To Father Peter Amaladoss Arockiam

and Father Michael J. Salvagna, CP —

With deep gratitude and abiding respect, I dedicate this work to you.

Father Peter, your words of mercy in the confessional helped restore a broken heart and set it on the path of healing. You saw past the labels the world assigned and reminded me of who I truly am in Christ— loved, forgiven, and called.

Father Michael, your gentle guidance, unwavering patience, and quiet strength have been a steady light in dark and uncertain places. You have been a shepherd, mentor, and true friend on this journey.

To both of you, thank you for being priests after the heart of Christ. This book—and the soul behind it—exists because of your prayers, witness, and love.

With gratitude beyond words,

John Henry

Introduction: Why the Papacy Still Matters

For nearly two thousand years, the papacy has stood at the heart of the Catholic Church's identity and controversy. No office in Christianity has drawn more scrutiny, reverence, resistance, or misunderstanding than that of the Bishop of Rome—whom Catholics recognize as the successor to St. Peter, the "rock" upon which Christ built His Church.

Among Protestants, the very idea of a pope is often seen as a corruption of early Christianity. For many, the papacy represents a departure from the simplicity of the Gospel—a political institution layered in centuries of tradition, pomp, and power, far removed from the humble Galilean carpenter who said, "Call no man father." They point to medieval scandals, inquisitions, and claims of infallibility as evidence that the papacy is not merely unnecessary—it's dangerous. For these Christians, the Reformation was not just a protest but a rescue.

Among the Eastern Orthodox, the critique is more complicated and, in many ways, more painful. Unlike Protestants, the Orthodox Church reveres apostolic tradition, liturgical beauty, and sacramental theology. They too honor the early Church Fathers and hold the ancient ecumenical councils in high esteem. Yet they accuse Rome of overreaching. They believe the pope once had a "primacy of honor" —a respected elder among equals—but over time claimed more power than he was ever meant to wield. In their eyes, the Great Schism of 1054 was not a rebellion, but a preservation of authentic apostolic governance. To this day, many Orthodox Christians see the pope as a sincere but mistaken brother—leading a Church that, while venerable, has lost its balance.

And even among Catholics, the papacy is sometimes misunderstood. Some imagine the pope as a kind of oracle who speaks directly for God. Others recoil at papal authority, afraid it means blind obedience to every decision or opinion expressed from the Vatican. Scandals involving popes, bishops, and bureaucracies only further complicate the conversation.

But what if the papacy is not what many imagine it to be?

What if it's not about imperial control, but humble stewardship?

What if its roots are not in medieval power struggles or political ambition, but in Scripture itself?

What if, far from being an invention of the fourth century, the role of the pope is the natural outgrowth of the Church Jesus established in the first?

And what if the enduring office of the Bishop of Rome is not a threat to unity—but the very instrument Christ gave to preserve it?

This book is an attempt to answer those questions—not with defensiveness or triumphalism, but with clarity and honesty. The papacy is not without its struggles. Its history includes saints and sinners, visionaries and villains. But beneath the human frailty, there is something divine at work: a promise made by Jesus Himself. A promise that the gates of hell would not prevail against the Church He founded—and that He would give the keys of the kingdom to one who would serve as both rock and shepherd.

This is the story of that promise.

To understand the papacy, we must step back—not just to the Middle Ages or to the Council of Trent, but all the way back to Jerusalem, to Caesarea Philippi, and even to the royal courts of ancient Israel. The Catholic claim about the pope doesn't begin with Vatican City or even with Peter's martyrdom in Rome. It begins with a Jewish Messiah, a kingdom not of this world, and a declaration that one man would hold the keys. This is not a story of sudden invention but of organic development—how a visible office, rooted in Christ's words and modeled after ancient biblical structures, matured over time to meet the needs of a growing, often divided, and sometimes wounded Church.

Even among practicing Catholics, the papacy can feel like a heavy subject. Some carry a quiet unease about certain decisions, public statements, or the political dynamics that occasionally swirl around the Vatican. Others find themselves defending the pope out of loyalty but not always with clarity. And for many, the concept of papal authority has been shaped more by media headlines or awkward history lessons than by prayerful study or theological understanding. In today's polarized world, it's easy to reduce the pope to either a hero or a villain—when in reality, he is first and foremost a shepherd, charged with a daunting and sacred task: to guard the deposit of faith and to strengthen his brothers. Before we can defend the papacy, we need to understand it. Before we react to what it has become, we need to remember how and why it began.

The truth is, the reality of the papacy is not something the Church had to invent—it's something nailed in perfect form within the pages of Sacred Scripture. From the keys of the kingdom in Isaiah, to the bold proclamation at Caesarea Philippi, to the shepherding charge on the shores of Galilee, Scripture doesn't merely hint at the papacy

—it reveals it. It defines it. It paints a clear and consistent picture of what Christ established. And yet, because many of our Orthodox and Protestant brothers and sisters insist we leave Scripture behind in order to defend the papacy, we will do that too. Not to rely on weak tradition or blind sentiment, but to show—through history, testimony, and reason—that what was planted by Christ has grown faithfully, even through struggle, into what we now recognize as the office of Peter. We will examine the aggravations between bishops East and West, the voices of the Early Church Fathers, and the common rejections that echo through time. But we will begin where everything must begin—with the Word of God—and follow the story where it leads.

  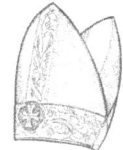

Chapter 1

The Keys of the Kingdom

The Call By The Sea

It began on the shore of a lake.

Simon was a fisherman—practical, rough-handed, probably up before sunrise most mornings, casting nets and reading the sky for signs of weather. His life was built on repetition, physical strength, and the patience it takes to work the sea. There was no indication that greatness would find him. And yet, one morning it did.

As Jesus walked along the Sea of Galilee, He saw Simon and his brother Andrew casting a net into the water. He called out, not with a sermon but with an invitation: *"Follow me, and I will make you fishers of men"* (Matthew 4:19). It was a call, but it was also a promise—one that would shape the rest of Simon's life. Jesus was speaking not only of mission but of identity. From the very beginning, He had plans for this man.

The Question at Caesarea Philippi

Years later, that plan would unfold more fully in the region of Caesarea Philippi—a region known for pagan worship and its great rock wall that loomed over a deep, dark crevice believed by locals to be a gateway to the underworld. This place, with its eerie legends and shrines to foreign gods, was not the sort of location one would expect for a moment of divine revelation. And yet, it was there that Jesus posed a question to His disciples that would alter the course of history.

"Who do you say that I am?" (Matthew 16:15)

The question came after the disciples had already shared what the crowds were saying—John the Baptist, Elijah, Jeremiah, or another of the prophets. But Jesus wasn't concerned with hearsay. He wanted to know what they believed. And Simon spoke.

"You are the Christ, the Son of the living God" (Matthew 16:16).

It was a moment of clarity, one not revealed to him by flesh and blood, as Jesus would say, but by the Father in heaven. In response, Jesus did what no rabbi or prophet had ever done before. He gave Simon a new name.

> *"You are Peter, and on this rock I will build my church, and the powers of death shall not prevail against it. I will give you the keys of the kingdom of heaven, and whatever you bind on earth shall be bound in heaven, and whatever you loose on earth shall be loosed in heaven"* (Matthew 16:18–19).

Kepha, Petros, and the Weight of a Name

This wasn't a gentle affirmation. It was a declaration. Jesus publicly renamed Simon—just as God had renamed Abram to Abraham and

Jacob to Israel. In the biblical tradition, a change of name marked a change of mission, a divine reorientation of a person's life. Here, Jesus names Simon *Kepha*, the Aramaic word for "rock." And what He says next reveals that the name is no symbolic flattery. Jesus identifies Peter as the foundation upon which He will build His Church.

The Gospel of Matthew, written in Greek, renders this name as *Petros* and then uses *petra* for the word "rock." Critics often seize on this shift, suggesting that *Petros* means a small stone while *petra* refers to a large rock. The implication, especially in some Protestant interpretations, is that Jesus was calling Peter a pebble—distinct from the real foundation, which they claim is either Jesus Himself or Peter's confession of faith.

But this argument collapses when one considers both the language and the context. In first-century Koine Greek, *Petros* and *petra* were often used interchangeably. More importantly, the distinction was imposed by the limitations of Greek grammar, not by theology. The feminine noun *petra* could not be used as a man's name. *Petros* is simply the masculine form needed to convey "rock" in reference to a male individual.

In Aramaic—the language Jesus actually spoke—the sentence would have contained no such distinction. It would have been: *"You are Kepha, and on this Kepha I will build my Church."* The repetition is unmistakable. The emphasis is deliberate. Jesus was not playing with metaphors. He was appointing a man and naming him in the process.

Standing Before the Gates of Hell

The significance of this moment deepens when one considers where it took place. Jesus brought the disciples to Caesarea Philippi—a region dominated by pagan imagery and a cliffside cave believed to be the very threshold of the underworld, commonly referred to as the "gates of Hades." It was in front of this backdrop that Jesus declared His Church would be built on Peter, and that *"the powers of death shall not prevail against it."* The symbolism could not have been more pointed. The Church would not merely survive evil—it would outlast it.

And then came the keys.

The Keys of the Kingdom

"I will give you the keys of the kingdom of heaven."

In ancient Israel, keys were not symbolic trinkets. They signified real authority—governmental authority—particularly over the royal household. To give someone the keys was to entrust him with responsibility and power. That's why Jesus didn't stop at the image of a rock. He handed Peter the language of office and governance. Binding and loosing were terms used in rabbinic Judaism to denote authoritative teaching and juridical decision-making. Peter is not merely a figure of faith—he is being commissioned.

And all of it—his name, his role, his authority—is directed to him personally. The Greek text uses second-person singular pronouns. *I will give you... whatever you bind... whatever you loose.* Jesus is not addressing the apostles as a group. This is a private commissioning made public, a singular appointment heard by the others.

Some would argue that this moment is exaggerated by Catholic interpretation—that Peter was simply first among equals, or that the rock Jesus referred to was something other than Peter himself. But if that were so, the entire structure of the passage would collapse under its own symbolism. Jesus does not change Simon's name only to call him insignificant. He does not hand him keys only to imply that they are decorative. He does not speak of gates that will not prevail while appointing a man too weak to stand.

Peter would fail, of course. He would deny Christ in the courtyard. He would return to fishing in despair. But failure is not the same as disqualification. Jesus would restore him on another shore, with another threefold encounter. And He would tell him then what was already evident here: *"Feed my sheep"* (cf. John 21:15–17).

The pattern is consistent. From the call beside the sea, to the name change at Caesarea Philippi, to the commission to shepherd, Jesus is not experimenting. He is establishing something lasting—something that will extend beyond Peter's life and take root in the Church He is founding.

A Steward in the Line of David

To fully understand what Jesus is doing here, we need to go backward in time—to another kingdom, another steward, and another set of keys. Because Jesus isn't speaking out of novelty. He is drawing from something deeply familiar to His Jewish audience. Something written centuries before in the scroll of the prophet Isaiah.

But Jesus's words about keys and binding were not unfamiliar phrases pulled from the air. They carried historical weight—echoes of an ancient office that every Jew in His audience would have recognized. To understand what Jesus was doing, we must look back to the days of the Davidic kingdom and a striking passage in the book of the prophet Isaiah.

> *"In that day I will call my servant Eliakim the son of Hilkiah, and I will clothe him with your robe, and will bind your girdle on him, and will commit your authority to his hand; and he shall be a father to the inhabitants of Jerusalem and to the house of Judah. And I will place on his shoulder the key of the house of David; he shall open, and none shall shut; and he shall shut, and none shall open"* (Isaiah 22:20–22).

This passage describes a royal appointment—Eliakim being named as steward over the house of David. In the monarchy of ancient Israel, the king could not manage every detail of governance himself. A steward, or prime minister, acted with delegated authority in the king's name. He had the king's trust, the king's robe, and—most notably—the *key* to the house.

The imagery is unmistakable. The steward is not the king, but he exercises royal authority. The key placed upon his shoulder is a visible sign of office. His decisions—what he opens, what he shuts—carry legal weight. His role is not symbolic. It is executive.

And this is precisely the image Jesus draws upon in Matthew 16 when He says to Peter, *"I will give you the keys of the kingdom of heaven."* The language is nearly identical. The connection is deliberate. Jesus is establishing His kingdom—the Kingdom of God—and as the Son of David, the eternal King, He is appointing a steward to govern in His name. Just as Eliakim was given the key to the house of David, Peter is given the keys to the Kingdom of Heaven.

But unlike Eliakim, Peter receives something more. He is not merely clothed in robes or handed earthly power—he is given a divine promise. *"The gates of hell shall not prevail against it."*

No Old Testament steward, no royal official, was ever promised such permanence or spiritual protection. Eliakim's authority was real, but temporary. In fact, just a few verses later, Isaiah prophesies his fall: *"In that day, says the Lord of hosts, the peg that was fastened in a secure place will give way, and it will be cut down and fall"* (Isaiah 22:25). The authority was great, but it was vulnerable—subject to human weakness and political instability.

Peter's role is different. Though he too is a flawed man, the office he receives is secured not by human stability, but by divine guarantee. Jesus doesn't merely give him the keys—He binds the office itself to heaven. *"Whatever you bind on earth shall be bound in heaven."* This is language of continuity, of succession, of divine oversight.

The parallels between Isaiah 22 and Matthew 16 are not coincidental. They are covenantal. Jesus, the new Davidic king, is restoring and transforming the structure of the old kingdom. But He is not replacing it with chaos or decentralization. He is fulfilling it with new authority—authority rooted in heaven, expressed on earth, and anchored in a visible, living office.

And so the steward of the kingdom is once again named and entrusted. But this time, the kingdom is not a geopolitical nation. It is the Church. The authority is not over land, but over souls. And the key is not to a palace in Jerusalem, but to the Kingdom of God.

Voices in Conversation

The Catholic interpretation of Matthew 16 and Isaiah 22 may seem bold to some—too certain, too hierarchical, too structured. But it is not a lonely claim. Even scholars outside the Catholic tradition have acknowledged the weight of these passages and the powerful continuity between Jesus' words to Peter and the language of royal office found in Isaiah.

Voices from the Outside: Protestant and Orthodox Reflections

R.T. France (1938–2012), an Anglican New Testament scholar, wrote in his commentary on the Gospel of Matthew:

"The image of the keys is most naturally explained in the light of Isaiah 22:22... Peter is to be the steward of the house of the Lord, given plenipotentiary authority to make decisions in the affairs of the kingdom."

— *The Gospel of Matthew* (New International Commentary on the New Testament)

The term "plenipotentiary" may seem dense, but it simply refers to one who has full power to act on behalf of another. In this case, France—though not Catholic—acknowledges that Peter is being granted true governing authority, not just symbolic leadership.

Craig S. Keener (b. 1960), a Protestant evangelical scholar, also comments on the gravity of Jesus' words:

"Jesus' promise to give Peter the 'keys of the kingdom' probably alludes to the steward's keys in Isaiah 22:22… Such keys imply delegated authority."

— *The IVP Bible Background Commentary: New Testament*

Jaroslav Pelikan (1923–2006), a Lutheran who later entered the Orthodox Church, offered this sober reflection on the papacy in his magisterial work *The Riddle of Roman Catholicism*:

"The Roman Church has a historical claim that no other church can make… its bishopric has an unbroken succession from Peter in a way no other sees itself connected to apostolic roots."

— *The Riddle of Roman Catholicism*

And Bishop Kallistos (Timothy) Ware (1934–2022), a leading Orthodox theologian, once stated:

"Rome was, and still is, the senior Church… The Pope's primacy was acknowledged, although understood differently. What was questioned was not the *fact* of his primacy, but its *extent*."

— *The Orthodox Church*

Even those who do not accept the Catholic view of the papacy acknowledge that Peter was given something real—and that Rome's claim did not arise out of nowhere.

Voices from the Heart of the Church: Catholic Reflections Across Time

The Early Church Fathers—those closest to the apostles—echoed what we've seen in Scripture.

St. Irenaeus (c. 130–202), bishop of Lyons and disciple of Polycarp (who had known the Apostle John), wrote:

"With this church [Rome], because of its superior origin, all churches must agree... for in her the apostolic tradition has always been preserved."

— *Against Heresies*, 3.3.2

St. Leo the Great (c. 400–461), Pope and Doctor of the Church, declared:

"The care of the universal Church should converge toward Peter's one seat, and nothing anywhere should be separated from its head."

— *Sermon 3: On His Installation*

Centuries later, St. Thomas Aquinas (1225–1274) would affirm:

"The pope, who is the successor of Peter, is the visible head of the whole Church, in whom the authority of Christ Himself remains present."

— *Summa Theologiae*, Suppl. Q.40, A.6

And in our own time, Pope St. John Paul II (1920–2005) emphasized in *Ut Unum Sint*:

"The Church needs her Shepherd to be a perpetual and visible source and foundation of unity."

Dr. Scott Hahn, a former Presbyterian minister turned Catholic theologian, reflects on Matthew 16 and Isaiah 22 with characteristic clarity:

"Jesus doesn't quote Scripture casually. When He talks about keys and authority, He's invoking a dynasty—the Davidic kingdom. And He's restoring it in His Church."

And as Bishop Robert Barron has often said:

"The Petrine office is not about power, but about unity. It is a ministry of service—of holding the Church together in the truth handed down by Christ."

Conclusion

What emerges from these reflections—Catholic, Protestant, and Orthodox alike—is not confusion but clarity. Jesus chose Peter. He gave him a name. He gave him keys. He established something visible and lasting.

The interpretations differ in tone and emphasis, but the central facts are remarkably consistent: Peter was appointed. He received real authority. And the Church that traces her lineage to him continues to bear that commission to this day.

As we move forward into the Acts of the Apostles and the witness of the early Church, the question is not whether Peter was chosen—but whether the office he was given remains active through his successors. The next chapter will begin to answer that.

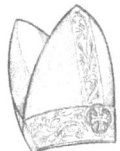  

Chapter 2

Called to Strengthen and Shepherd

The Power to Bind and Loose

Before Peter stepped forward at Pentecost or led the apostles at the Council of Jerusalem, Jesus had already entrusted him with something extraordinary. Standing in the shadow of pagan temples at Caesarea Philippi, Jesus said to him alone, *"Whatever you bind on earth shall be bound in heaven, and whatever you loose on earth shall be loosed in heaven"* (Matthew 16:19). The words were direct, singular, and unmistakable. Peter, the one who had confessed Jesus as the Christ, was being given divine authority with heavenly consequences.

This phrase—binding and loosing—carried legal and spiritual weight in Jewish tradition. It referred to the authority to make judgments, to interpret the law, and to include or exclude individuals from the covenant community. In other words, it was the language of leadership. And Jesus applies it not generally, but specifically—to Peter.

Yet later in Matthew's Gospel, a similar phrase appears again: *"Truly, I say to you, whatever you bind on earth shall be bound in heaven, and whatever you loose on earth shall be loosed in heaven"* (Matthew 18:18). This time, He is speaking to all the apostles. The authority is extended, but it is crucial to notice that the extension comes *after* Peter has already been singled out and appointed as the rock. Peter receives the keys in Matthew 16. The others share in the authority of binding and loosing in Matthew 18. The foundation is not diluted. Rather, it is reinforced and broadened to support the Church that is beginning to take shape.

Protestants and Orthodox often point to this moment to argue that Peter held no authority above the others. They say the keys are symbolic, the rock is faith, and the authority is equal. But Matthew's Gospel does not present the events in that way. The chronology matters. The keys are not given to a group. They are given to a person. The authority is real, and it begins with Peter. That it is later shared does not weaken the uniqueness of his role. In fact, it mirrors the logic of stewardship and service. Peter is the one who receives the commission first because he is the one who must lead. That leadership includes collaboration, but it is not eclipsed by it.

Even the favored phrase "first among equals" requires careful scrutiny. It sounds egalitarian. It gives a sense of shared responsibility. But in any structured body, being first among equals still means something. A lead bishop among bishops, a chairperson among colleagues, a chief among captains—all hold a role that sets direction and anchors unity. If the apostles were equals in every way, why single Peter out at all? Why change his name? Why speak to him directly? Why pray for him uniquely?

Strengthen Your Brethren

One of the most illuminating moments of Peter's distinct role comes quietly in Luke's Gospel. At the Last Supper, Jesus turns to Peter and says, *"Simon, Simon, behold, Satan demanded to have you, that he might sift you like wheat, but I have prayed for you that your faith may not fail; and when you have turned again, strengthen your brethren"* (Luke 22:31–32). In English, the richness of this passage can be overlooked, but the original Greek offers a striking insight. When Jesus says *"Satan demanded to have you,"* the word *"you"* is plural—referring to all the apostles. But when He says, *"I have prayed for you,"* the word shifts to singular. Jesus intercedes for Peter personally, not to the exclusion of the others, but so that Peter may in turn strengthen them.

This moment, occurring just before Peter's denial, reinforces the reality of his human weakness. But it also clarifies his mission. Jesus is not replacing Peter after his failure—He is preparing him to rise from it. Peter's leadership is not built on personal perfection. It is built on grace, on the commission of Christ, and on the power of repentance. When Jesus says, *"strengthen your brethren,"* He is giving Peter a mandate not just to return, but to lead.

The context makes this all the more powerful. Jesus knows Peter will fall. He knows the rooster will crow. And still He speaks of a future moment when Peter will be the one to support the others. That is not the language of someone being quietly sidelined. It is the language of someone being refined, tested, and called.

The Shepherd and His Steward

If there was ever a metaphor that revealed both the heart and mission of God, it is the image of the shepherd. From the earliest pages of Scripture, the Lord identifies Himself as the one who watches, guides, protects, and seeks His people—not with the indifference of a distant ruler, but with the intimacy of a shepherd among his sheep.

The psalmist cries, *"The Lord is my shepherd, I shall not want"* (Psalm 23:1). Isaiah proclaims, *"He will feed his flock like a shepherd; he will gather the lambs in his arms"* (Isaiah 40:11). Through the prophet Ezekiel, God expresses both frustration with Israel's corrupt leaders and His own promise to act in their place: *"Behold, I, I myself will search for my sheep and will seek them out"* (Ezekiel 34:11). He continues: *"I will rescue them from all places where they have been scattered... I will feed them with good pasture... I myself will be the shepherd of my sheep"* (Ezekiel 34:12–15).

This divine declaration is not poetic posturing. It is a promise—a prophecy that God Himself will one day take up the shepherd's staff.

And so, centuries later, when Jesus declares, *"I am the good shepherd. The good shepherd lays down his life for the sheep"* (John 10:11), He is not merely offering a gentle analogy. He is fulfilling the very promise of Ezekiel 34. He is the Lord who has come in the flesh to tend His flock. He is the One who sees the people as *"harassed and helpless, like sheep without a shepherd"* (Matthew 9:36), and in response, He steps into the field Himself. He calls His own by name. He knows them, and they follow Him (John 10:3–4).

And yet, at the close of His earthly ministry, the Good Shepherd does something extraordinary. He hands the flock to another.

On the shores of Galilee, beside a charcoal fire and after a shared meal, the risen Jesus addresses Simon Peter directly:

"Simon, son of John, do you love me more than these?... Feed my lambs... Tend my sheep... Feed my sheep" (John 21:15–17).

The repetition is not arbitrary. Neither are the verbs. The Greek terms used—*boskō* ("feed") and *poimainō* ("tend" or "shepherd")—carry weight. They imply real responsibility, real authority, and a share in the mission of the true Shepherd. The word *poimainō* in particular is used elsewhere in Scripture to describe governing or leading with divine mandate (cf. Revelation 2:27). Jesus is not simply asking Peter to love. He is commissioning him to lead.

This moment has often been reduced to a scene of forgiveness—as if Jesus is merely restoring Peter after his threefold denial. But something far deeper is happening. Jesus, the Shepherd prophesied by Ezekiel, now entrusts His sheep to Peter. He does not give this commission to the group. He does not ask all the apostles to shepherd. He speaks to *Peter alone.*

This is not a contradiction of Christ's role as the true Shepherd. Peter is not being asked to replace Jesus, but to *steward His flock* in His name. This is precisely how Peter himself understands the task. Later, writing to fellow elders, he exhorts them to *"shepherd the flock of God that is among you,"* and he refers to Jesus as the *"chief Shepherd"* who will appear in glory (1 Peter 5:2–4). Peter's role is visible. It is earthly. But it is always in service to the One who remains the head of the Church.

In Peter, we see the visible shepherd appointed by the invisible Shepherd. The echo of Ezekiel, the fulfillment in Christ, and the apostolic continuity all converge in this moment on the Galilean shore. The one who had once faltered is now entrusted with the care of the entire flock. And the language Christ uses is unmistakably pastoral: lambs and sheep, feeding and tending.

It is also worth noting the setting. Jesus could have chosen any place to deliver this commission, but He chose the Sea of Galilee—where it all began. It was on this same sea that Peter was first called to leave his nets and follow (cf. Matthew 4:18–19). Now, having passed through denial, repentance, and renewal, Peter is called again—this time not to fish, but to shepherd.

In this, the arc of Peter's vocation becomes clear. He is not merely an apostle. He is the *shepherd-apostle.* And while others will share in apostolic mission, only Peter receives the direct mandate to feed and tend the flock of Christ.

The Shepherd has spoken. And He has chosen a steward.

Points of Objection and Points of Agreement

When Catholics speak of Peter's unique authority—his power to bind and loose, and his role as shepherd—many non-Catholic Christians raise sincere and thoughtful objections. These challenges often stem not from rejecting Scripture, but from reading it through a different theological lens. Engaging with these differences charitably can bring deeper clarity to what Jesus actually entrusted to Peter—and why it matters.

Some Protestant scholars, for example, accept that Jesus gave Peter the *"keys of the kingdom of heaven"* (Matthew 16:19), but argue that this authority was not exclusive to him. They often point to Matthew 18:18, where Jesus says to the wider group of apostles, *"Whatever you bind on earth shall be bound in heaven, and whatever you loose on earth shall be loosed in heaven."* From this, it is argued that Peter's authority is not unique, but shared.

While it's true that Jesus later extends the language of binding and loosing to all the apostles, the order and imagery remain significant. Peter receives this authority first—and he alone is given the *keys*. The symbol of the keys does not appear again in Matthew 18. Instead, it evokes a separate and royal image drawn from Isaiah 22:22: the keys of the house of David, placed on the shoulder of a steward who governs on the king's behalf. In biblical thought, keys do not represent shared access. They represent *delegated governance*. That Jesus singles out Peter for this image suggests something more than symbolic inclusion.

Some theologians suggest that Matthew 18 presents not a flattening of authority, but a *structured sharing*—where Peter's role remains foundational, yet the others participate in it under his visible leadership. In this sense, Peter is not isolated above the others, but serves as the center of visible unity and judgment. His binding and loosing carry the weight of a steward's office, not simply a preacher's boldness.

Objections also arise when Catholics point to Peter's role as shepherd. Protestants and Orthodox alike emphasize that Christ alone is the Good Shepherd (John 10:11), and that all Christian leaders are called to care for the flock. The idea of *one man* being singled out as "the shepherd" may feel forced or even unbiblical. In their view, Jesus' command to Peter in John 21—*"Feed my lambs... Tend my sheep... Feed my sheep"*—is seen as a personal restoration after Peter's denial, not a public commissioning of singular authority.

But a deeper reading suggests otherwise. The Greek verbs Jesus uses —*boskō* and *poimainō*—are not limited to pastoral gestures. The latter, especially, carries a connotation of *ruling* or *governing*, as in Revelation 2:27: "He shall rule [*poimainō*] them with a rod of iron." Peter is not simply being consoled. He is being commissioned to *govern* the flock in Christ's name.

This interpretation is affirmed not only by Catholic voices, but by several respected Protestant scholars. Lutheran theologian Oscar Cullmann wrote: *"Peter is the representative of the one Church and the visible head of the disciples. He is the shepherd appointed by Christ."* Though Cullmann rejected certain Catholic doctrines about the papacy, he clearly acknowledged Peter's distinct and visible pastoral mission.

Similarly, F.F. Bruce (1910–1990), a highly regarded Evangelical scholar, noted that while all the apostles share in Christ's mission, Peter is "prominent in the Gospels and Acts" because he is "the first among his equals, and often the spokesman for the rest." Though Bruce emphasizes collegiality, he does not deny Peter's pastoral leadership. Rather, he recognizes its functional reality in the life of the early Church.

From the Orthodox tradition, St. John Chrysostom reflects deeply on Christ's command to Peter in John 21. He writes: *"Peter, do you love me more than these? Feed my sheep." Why did He not say this to the others? Because Peter was fervent and the chief of the apostles.* (cf. *Homily 88 on John*). Chrysostom's interpretation reflects a recognition—not of tyranny—but of *delegated responsibility*, born of love and visible leadership.

To be clear, none of these scholars suggest that Peter is infallible in his person, nor that his authority excludes the voice of the broader apostolic body. But what they *do* acknowledge is this: Peter's role was *distinct*. His reception of the keys was *unique*. His commissioning to feed the sheep was *singular*. And even within communities that do not accept the full Catholic doctrine of the papacy, these distinctions are not always denied. They are often admitted—just not followed to their fullest conclusion.

What emerges is a picture of authority that is personal, pastoral, and representative. Peter is not only called to confess. He is called to bind, to loose, and to shepherd. He is given the responsibility to govern and guide—not instead of Christ, but in service to Him. And this, precisely, is the Catholic claim.

The Logic of Continuity

What becomes clear, even to those who question the Catholic position, is that Peter's commission was not symbolic or sentimental. It was substantial. He was given keys, entrusted with the flock, and empowered to bind and loose in a way that directly affected both earth and heaven. These were not honorary gestures. They were governing responsibilities.

And this governing role—established by Christ Himself—was not given in a vacuum. It was part of a plan. Christ was preparing His Church, not for a single generation, but for the centuries to come. If

Peter's role as steward, judge, and shepherd was necessary when the Church was small and vulnerable, how much more necessary would that visible leadership be as the Church grew, spread, and encountered internal and external threats?

It is not unreasonable, then, to ask: *If Peter's authority was essential in the first century, why would it cease to be so afterward?* If Christ built His Church upon a rock, and that rock was Peter, then it follows that the structure built upon him was meant to endure. Not as a tribute to Peter the man, but as a continuation of the mission Christ entrusted to him.

Even those who hesitate to affirm the Catholic claim often admit the clarity of Peter's role in the Gospels. What is harder to deny is the logic that follows. The Catholic Church has not invented something beyond Peter. It has preserved what began with him. And what began with him was an office—established by Christ, guided by the Spirit, and handed down in succession—meant to shepherd the people of God across nations, cultures, and centuries.

Chapter 3

A Church for All Nations

The Catholic Mission and the Spirit of Truth

Long before the Spirit descended at Pentecost, long before Peter stood to preach or the apostles scattered to the corners of the empire, Jesus had already laid out the shape of His Church. Not as a loose network of believers or an underground movement of spiritual individualists—but as a body, a household, a kingdom. Its scope would be global. Its teaching would be consistent. Its unity would be visible. And its endurance would be guaranteed by divine promise.

Standing on a hillside in Galilee, the risen Christ gave His disciples their marching orders:

> *"All authority in heaven and on earth has been given to me. Go therefore and make disciples of all nations... teaching them to observe all that I have commanded you; and lo, I am with you always, to the close of the age"* (Matthew 28:18–20).

This was no small commission. It was not regional, temporary, or symbolic. It was *catholic* in the truest sense—universal in mission, total in scope, enduring through time. The word *catholic* comes from the Greek *katholikos*, meaning *according to the whole*. From the very beginning, Christ's Church was meant to speak to the whole of humanity, preserve the whole of His teaching, and remain whole in its visible unity.

And here is where the Catholic reading of Scripture becomes not only logical, but necessary. A Church with a worldwide mission cannot survive on sentiment. It cannot depend on scattered interpretation or individual authority. It requires what Christ explicitly provides: teaching, structure, stewardship, and the abiding presence of the Spirit.

Jesus does not tell the apostles to "share their impressions" or "spread inspiration." He commands them to *teach*—not selectively, but comprehensively: *"all that I have commanded you."* He does not say, "until the generation passes," but *"to the close of the age."* The blueprint of the Church is already present here: apostolic authority, doctrinal fidelity, and perpetual mission.

These are not elements to be assembled later in Church councils or Roman offices. They are embedded in the words of Christ Himself. The apostles are not simply messengers—they are *guardians* of what has been handed on, called to preserve and proclaim a deposit of truth that is not theirs to alter.

To make such a mission possible, Jesus gives not only instructions, but an *interior guide*. Before His Passion, He promised the apostles:

"When the Spirit of truth comes, he will guide you into all the truth..." (John 16:13).

This guidance is not vague intuition. It is not private revelation. It is a promise made to the apostolic body—that the truth they teach will not come from themselves, but from the Spirit. The Spirit does not bypass the Church. He speaks through it. He does not lead each person into an individual understanding of truth. He ensures that the Church itself remains the pillar and foundation of truth (cf. 1 Timothy 3:15).

And again, the structure is already in place: Christ calls, commissions, and empowers the apostles. He ensures that they are taught from within by the Spirit. And He remains with them always, not as an idea, but as a presence—binding heaven and earth in the very act of their mission.

What begins in the Gospels is not a spiritual abstraction. It is a real Church. And the Church that Jesus promises—one that teaches, governs, forgives, feeds, and perseveres—is already unfolding before the first page of Acts is ever turned.

The Catholic reading of Scripture does not import this vision from tradition. It draws it from the very words of Christ. The Church is not an afterthought. It is the fruit of His mission. And the authority He gives to Peter, the command He gives to the apostles, and the promise of the Spirit together reveal a design far greater than any human plan.

This is the Church that will speak in many tongues at Pentecost, that will send missionaries across empires, that will hold councils to settle disputes, that will baptize believers in every generation. This is the Church that Christ founded. This is the Church He promised to remain with always.

And this is the Church we still see today.

Catholic in Mission - Orthodox in Teaching

And perhaps what's most important to recognize is that the defining feature of the Catholic Church has never been her title—it's always been her *mission*. The word *catholic* comes from the Greek *katholikos*, meaning *universal* or *according to the whole*. From the beginning, the Church Christ established was called to go to the whole world, teach the whole Gospel, and invite the whole of humanity into communion with God.

That's why, as early as A.D. 107, St. Ignatius of Antioch, a disciple of the apostle John, would write: *"Wherever Jesus Christ is, there is the Catholic Church"* (*Letter to the Smyrnaeans*, 8:2). At the time, he wasn't defending an institution or naming a denomination—those didn't yet exist. He was describing the visible, united Church that remained in communion with the apostles and preserved the faith they had handed on.

As the Church grew and the Gospel spread across cultures, new questions emerged. So did new errors. Some were sincere misunderstandings about Christ's nature or the Trinity. Others were serious departures from apostolic teaching. In response, the Church began to articulate more clearly what she had always believed. The term *catholic*—once simply descriptive—became an identifier. The Church had to distinguish herself from groups that claimed the name of Christ but rejected the fullness of what He taught.

It's no coincidence that from the earliest centuries, the Church was recognized by two essential marks: *orthodoxy* and *catholicity*. She was *orthodox* in her teaching—faithful to the truth entrusted by Christ to the apostles. And she was *catholic* in her mission—sent to all peoples, not confined by ethnicity, language, or region. This identity existed *long before Constantine*, long before ecumenical councils gave formal definitions. The Church was already visible, already authoritative, already on mission—because Christ Himself had designed her that way.

In the chapters ahead, we'll see how this identity begins to take fuller shape—not through political power, but through preaching, persecution, and the power of the Holy Spirit. The Catholic Church did not arise from the ambitions of emperors. She arose from the promises of Christ—promises made before a single sermon was preached in Acts, and before a single letter of the New Testament had been written.

And at the center of this unfolding mission still stands Peter—the one who was given the keys, the one who was told to strengthen his brethren, the one who was called to feed the sheep. The promises of Christ were not scattered. They were entrusted to apostles and centered in one man, the Rock. The Church was being prepared—not for disintegration, but for unity. Not for obscurity, but for mission. And Peter, frail yet chosen, would be the one to rise first when the Spirit came and the Church found her voice.

Voices That Affirm the Mission

The Catholic reading of Scripture is not built on isolated proof texts or theological creativity. It is the fruit of continuity—drawn from the words of Christ, carried out by the apostles, and affirmed by the earliest generations of believers.

As early as A.D. 107, St. Ignatius of Antioch, a disciple of the apostle John, wrote plainly, *"Wherever Jesus Christ is, there is the Catholic Church"* (*Letter to the Smyrnaeans*, 8:2). At a time when Christians were still persecuted and the New Testament was not yet fully compiled, Ignatius already spoke of a visible, united, and identifiable Church—one rooted in the apostles and in communion with their successors.

This was not a political development. It was the fruit of fidelity. St. Irenaeus, writing in the second century, echoed this idea: *"Where the Church is, there is the Spirit of God; and where the Spirit of God is, there is the Church and every kind of grace"* (*Against Heresies*, Book 3.24.1). For these early witnesses, the Church was not invisible or amorphous. It was a body with clear teaching, sacramental life, and apostolic structure—sent to all nations and safeguarded by divine promise.

Even Protestant and non-Catholic scholars have acknowledged this continuity. The Reformed scholar D.A. Carson, while not Catholic, affirms that *"the Great Commission is not merely evangelistic; it is didactic. It involves teaching converts everything Jesus commanded."* He emphasizes that this implies *a community capable of preserving and transmitting that teaching in full*. Similarly, R.T. France describes the authority given in Matthew 28 as *"comprehensive and enduring,"* noting that the commission implies more than momentary leadership—it implies stewardship of truth for the long term.

On the promise of the Holy Spirit, the late evangelical theologian Craig Keener observes that *"the Spirit's guidance into all truth was not a license for individuals to invent theology, but a corporate promise to the apostolic foundation of the Church."* Even outside Catholic tradition, there is acknowledgment that Jesus entrusted His teaching to a visible, continuing community—not to fragmentation or personal interpretation.

Catholic voices, too, have long affirmed that the Church's universality is not accidental—it is essential. Joseph Ratzinger, before becoming Pope Benedict XVI, wrote: *"The Church was not made Catholic by expansion; it was Catholic from the first moment."* That insight echoes what we have already seen: the Church's mission to all nations, her teaching of the full Gospel, and her unity under apostolic authority were not later developments—they were present in Christ's very commission.

These voices, drawn from East and West, ancient and modern, Catholic and non-Catholic, bear witness to the same truth: the Church Christ founded was meant to last, to teach, and to reach the world. That Church is not an idea. It is a body. And its foundation—Christ Himself—remains unshaken.

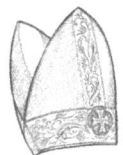  

Chapter 4

The Rock Speaks

Peter, Pentecost, and the Birth of the Church

They waited. Not in fear, but in obedience. The risen Christ had commanded them to remain in Jerusalem until they were *"clothed with power from on high"* (Luke 24:49). And so, in the Upper Room, they prayed. They gathered. They waited. The apostles—along with Mary, the mother of Jesus—stood between promise and fulfillment, between memory and mission.

Then, on the feast of Pentecost, the waiting ended.

 "When the day of Pentecost had come, they were all together in one place. And suddenly a sound came from heaven like the rush of a mighty wind... and there appeared to them tongues as of fire, distributed and resting on each one of them. And they were all filled with the Holy Spirit..." (Acts 2:1–4)

The Church was born—not in silence, but in sound. Not in theory, but in fire. And it was not a private moment for personal renewal. It was a public anointing for global mission. The Spirit of Truth had come, just as Jesus had promised. But now came the question: *Who would speak?*

The answer, as always, was Peter.

"But Peter, standing with the eleven, lifted up his voice..." (Acts 2:14)

It is no small detail that Peter rises first. He does not merely join the others—he stands apart, though never alone. He speaks not as a volunteer, but as one appointed. The same Peter who had been given the keys now opens the door to the kingdom. The same Peter who had once denied Christ now proclaims Him boldly. And the same Peter who had been told to "feed my sheep" now feeds them with the Word.

His sermon is not abstract or sentimental. It is deeply Scriptural, rooted in the prophet Joel, in the Psalms, and in the covenant promises fulfilled in Christ. But it is also piercing. Peter does not hesitate to confront the crowd with the reality of the Cross:

"This Jesus, delivered up according to the definite plan and foreknowledge of God, you crucified and killed... But God raised him up..." (Acts 2:23–24)

The impact is immediate. The people are "cut to the heart" and cry out, *"What shall we do?"* (Acts 2:37)

And Peter, again taking the lead, gives the first apostolic response:

"Repent, and be baptized every one of you in the name of Jesus Christ for the forgiveness of your sins; and you shall receive the gift of the Holy Spirit" (Acts 2:38)

This is not a spontaneous revival. It is the foundation of sacramental life. Baptism, repentance, and the gift of the Spirit—offered by the authority of the apostolic voice, and through the leadership of Peter.

That day, three thousand were baptized. The Church that Christ had promised was now visible, public, and growing. And at the head of this moment, as at the moment of commission, was Peter.

The Office Must Be Fierce

Peter may have been clothed in the Spirit, but the road ahead would demand more than bold preaching. It would require courage unto death. Every apostle except John would die a martyr. And Peter—the Rock—would one day be crucified upside down in Rome. The office entrusted to him was not ceremonial. It was a commission that would call for suffering, truth, and strength.

The papacy would carry that same burden through centuries of chaos, conflict, and conversion. At its best, it would preserve the Gospel with heroic fidelity. At its worst, it would reveal how easily power tempts even the anointed to forget what power is for. The history of the papacy is filled with holy men who suffered for the faith, and others who were distracted by pleasure, politics, or fear. But through it all, the Gospel was never compromised. The message of Christ—His life, death, and resurrection—was never erased or rewritten.

Even when Judas betrayed the Truth, and Peter denied the Truth out of fear, the Truth Himself remained. And He entrusted that truth to His Church—not to perfect men, but to a perfect promise: *"When the Spirit of truth comes, He will guide you into all the truth"* (John 16:13).

The consistency of human weakness has never faltered. But neither has the Holy Spirit.

The more any pope or bishop forgets the mission of the Church—to proclaim Christ, to teach the faith, and to love as He loved—the more space there is for scandal, division, and confusion. But when the office is rooted in service—when the one who holds the keys remembers that he is first a *servant of the servants of God*—then the Gospel shines with clarity, and the Church becomes a beacon to the nations.

Love God. Love one another. That is the heart of every sermon, from Peter at Pentecost to the present day—even in the mouths of popes whose personal lives were less than admirable. The Holy Spirit has never withdrawn. The message has never been lost. And that is what we must stay grounded in today.

The Presence They Knew

The earliest believers did not gather around ideas. They gathered around a Presence.

In the Acts of the Apostles, the community is described as devoting themselves to *"the apostles' teaching and fellowship, to the breaking of the bread and the prayers"* (Acts 2:42). The phrase *"the breaking of the bread"* may sound familiar—even casual—to modern ears. But in Greek, the phrase is τῇ κλάσει τοῦ ἄρτου (*tē klasei tou artou*), and its usage is anything but ordinary.

The word *klasis* (κλάσις), from *kláō* (κλάω), means "to break." It's not just tearing or sharing—it's the deliberate act of dividing bread, often in ritual or liturgical contexts. *Artos* (ἄρτος) means bread, but within Christian usage, it came to carry sacramental weight. Together, this phrase appears in a strikingly Eucharistic context—one that links directly back to Jesus' actions at the Last Supper: *"He took bread... broke it... and gave it..."* (cf. Luke 22:19).

This same wording is echoed in Luke 24:30–31, when the risen Jesus was *"made known to them in the breaking of the bread."* The disciples' eyes were opened not at the moment of walking or talking—but when He repeated the sacred pattern of blessing, breaking, and giving. That was the moment of recognition.

So when Acts uses *tē klasei tou artou*, it's not just describing a meal. It's a reference to the central liturgical act of the Church—what we now call the Eucharist. It was already more than a memorial. It was mystery. A mystery they may not have fully systematized in theological terms, but clearly recognized as sacred encounter.

Even Paul, writing in the early 50s A.D., affirms this reality:

"The cup of blessing that we bless, is it not a participation (koinōnia) in the blood of Christ? The bread that we break (klōmen), is it not a participation in the body of Christ?" (1 Corinthians 10:16)

And again, in warning the Church at Corinth, Paul says that to eat and drink unworthily is to *"profane the body and blood of the Lord"* (1 Corinthians 11:27). Such language only makes sense if the Eucharist truly is what Christ said: *"This is my body... this is my blood"* (Matthew 26:26–28).

The apostles may not have used the later theological term *transubstantiation*, but they lived the truth it conveys. From the moment of Pentecost onward, the breaking of the bread was the center of their worship and the source of their strength. They gathered not merely to recall—but to receive. The Church was Eucharistic from the beginning, and it still is today.

Peter Steps Forward

The same man who once trembled at the question of a servant girl now stands unshaken before a crowd of thousands.

In Acts 3, Peter and John approach the temple at the hour of prayer. At the gate called Beautiful, they encounter a man lame from birth. The man expects coins. What he receives is a miracle—and a message.

"*Silver and gold have I none, but what I have I give you: in the name of Jesus Christ of Nazareth, rise up and walk*" (Acts 3:6).

The Greek construction here—ἐν τῷ ὀνόματι Ἰησοῦ Χριστοῦ τοῦ Ναζωραίου (*en tō onomati Iēsou Christou tou Nazōraiou*)—carries legal and spiritual weight. To invoke a name "in the dative" like this is to act by the authority of that person. Peter is not offering a hopeful blessing. He is exercising the authority of Christ.

The miracle causes a stir, drawing the attention of crowds—and soon, the religious leaders. Peter seizes the moment, not for self-glory, but for proclamation:

"*Why do you stare at us, as though by our own power or piety we made him walk? The God of Abraham, Isaac, and Jacob... has glorified His servant Jesus...*" (Acts 3:12–13)

He goes further—boldly confronting the crowd with their complicity in Christ's death, but offering repentance and restoration:

"*Repent, therefore, and turn again, that your sins may be blotted out...*" (Acts 3:19)

These are not the words of a fearful man. These are the words of a shepherd leading his flock out of confusion and into truth.

When the temple authorities arrest Peter and John, Acts 4:8 tells us that Peter is "*filled with the Holy Spirit.*" The Greek is πλησθεὶς πνεύματος ἁγίου (*plēstheis pneumatos hagiou*)—not merely influenced, but inwardly filled to overflowing. This same Peter who denied Christ now testifies before the very council that condemned Him:

"*There is no other name under heaven given among men by which we must be saved*" (Acts 4:12).

Peter does not preach general truths. He proclaims *Jesus Christ crucified, risen, and reigning*. He does not hedge or hold back. He sets the tone for apostolic proclamation—not as a domineering monarch, but as a servant-leader empowered by Christ.

By Acts 5, the apostles are performing many signs and wonders. Yet it is Peter who again steps forward, both as a healer and a spiritual authority. People bring the sick into the streets hoping that "his shadow might fall on them" (Acts 5:15). This isn't superstition—it's recognition of grace operating through Peter in a unique way.

He also exercises moral authority in the startling case of Ananias and Sapphira. It is Peter who discerns their lie—not simply to men, but to the Holy Spirit—and who pronounces the judgment that follows. This moment reveals the weight of his office: not just as preacher or miracle-worker, but as one entrusted with guarding the integrity of the Church.

None of this negates the role of the other apostles. They too are preaching, healing, and leading. But Peter's visibility is intentional. He is not simply the most vocal—he is the one commissioned by Christ to strengthen his brothers (Luke 22:32), to feed the sheep (John 21:17), and to hold the keys (Matthew 16:19).

What we see in these chapters is not Peter *taking* power, but Peter *carrying* the mission he was given. The Holy Spirit animates the Church—but Peter is already serving as its visible anchor, pace-setter, and spokesman.

Priesthood: In Persona Christi

Peter's bold witness in these early chapters is more than leadership—it is sacramental in character. He speaks and acts not merely as a messenger, but as a vessel through whom Christ continues His ministry.

The Church later describes this mystery as *in persona Christi*—"in the person of Christ." But we do not need to wait for Latin vocabulary or conciliar language to see its meaning. It is already unfolding in the upper room, in the temple courts, and in the very breath of Christ.

"He breathed on them and said to them, 'Receive the Holy Spirit. If you forgive the sins of any, they are forgiven...'" (John 20:22–23)

This breath—*pneuma*—is the Spirit of the risen Lord, re-creating what sin destroyed. When Peter forgives, when Peter preaches, when Peter heals, it is not Peter alone. It is Christ, the eternal High Priest, acting through His chosen apostles. *"He who hears you hears Me"* (Luke 10:16) is not metaphor. It is the divine pattern of mediation.

This does not mean that Peter—or any priest—is necessary *instead of* Christ. It means that the priest is necessary *because of* Christ. The New Covenant ministerial priesthood is not a replacement for Jesus' saving work. It is the very way He *applies* that work to His people. Peter's leadership is not about rank. It is about representing the Shepherd to the flock (cf. John 21:17).

As the early Church will come to understand, the sacraments are not human ceremonies. They are divine encounters. When the Church teaches that priests act *in persona Christi*, she is not elevating the man. She is grounding the office in the One who fills it.

Through Peter and the apostles, we begin to see the shape of this priesthood—not in elaborate garments or human grandeur, but in servant-hearted leadership, courageous preaching, sacramental action, and radical dependence on the Holy Spirit.

This is what gives the Sacrament of Holy Orders its divine commission. Christ does not ask His followers to invent ministries or choose spiritual paths at random. He institutes a priesthood rooted in Himself. The priest does not forgive sins on his own. Christ forgives through him. The priest does not say, *"This is Christ's body,"* but *"This is My Body,"* because he is speaking not as himself, but in the person of the Son.

The New Covenant has its own altar, its own sacrifice, its own priesthood—not as a shadow of the old, but as its fulfillment. And at the heart of it stands Peter, not as a self-appointed chief, but as the one who received the breath, the commission, the keys, and the call to feed the sheep.

Apostolic Succession: A Living Continuity

The events of Acts are not isolated moments of divine intervention. They are the foundation of a living continuity—a Church both Spirit-filled and structured, mystical and visible, grounded in Scripture and safeguarded by shepherds.

What Catholics—and our Orthodox brothers and sisters—recognize as *apostolic succession* flows directly from the pattern Christ established. Jesus did not entrust His Gospel to scrolls alone. He entrusted it to men filled with the Holy Spirit, given authority to teach, govern, and sanctify in His name. This was not symbolic. It was incarnational. The Word became flesh—and the mission of the Word was carried forward through flesh-and-blood ministers.

Apostolic succession is not simply a lineage of names. It is the passing on of mission, grace, and authority through the laying on of hands and the breath of Christ. When the apostles laid hands on others, they were not transferring popularity or charisma. They were participating in Christ's priesthood, making sure that His presence and truth would endure in every generation.

This is why the early Church, as we will continue to see, took false teaching seriously and right teaching personally. The standard was not personal inspiration, but fidelity to the apostles' doctrine. And the succession of bishops, in communion with Peter's office, ensured that the Church would remain both one and holy—guarded not by mere men, but by the Holy Spirit working through them.

Peter's role here is not incidental. He does not act apart from the others, but he serves as their visible anchor—the one who speaks first, preaches boldly, discerns clearly, and strengthens the brethren. His voice will rise again in Acts 10, at Cornelius's house, as the Gospel breaks through to the Gentiles. And at the Council of Jerusalem in Acts 15, his discernment and testimony will again shape the path forward.

But first, we turn the page to see what happens next in the growing Church. Peter and the apostles will face increasing opposition, miraculous deliverances, and the remarkable story of Saul of Tarsus—a man who once hunted Christians, and will soon become their most passionate preacher.

The fire that was lit at Pentecost is spreading. The Rock is steady beneath their feet. The Church is alive.

Chapter 5

A Church that Does Not Die

When the final page of the Acts of the Apostles is turned, the story of the early Church doesn't end—it simply continues. It is tempting, even for Christians, to treat the Book of Acts as a powerful but isolated narrative—something beautiful in its infancy but long since buried under layers of history, scandal, division, and human error. But to think this way is to miss the truth that changes everything: the Church Christ founded is still alive. Still breathing. Still holy. Still apostolic.

It did not vanish when Peter and Paul were martyred. It did not dissolve when the last living apostle breathed his last. It did not fragment into a thousand pieces to be picked up and reimagined by later generations who "meant well." It continued—through structure, through succession, and through the very authority that Christ Himself gave to His apostles.

Apostolic Succession: The Lifeline of the Church

Christ did not establish a Church for one generation only. He promised, *"I am with you always, to the close of the age"* (Matt 28:20). And He fulfilled that promise by giving His authority to the apostles, who then passed it on—by prayer, by the laying on of hands, and by the guidance of the Holy Spirit—to those who would come after them.

This is what Catholics mean when we speak of apostolic succession. It is not a decorative tradition or a poetic theory. It is the essential mechanism by which the Church remains united to Christ. It ensures that the sacraments are valid. That the teaching office has authority. That the Church remains, in every generation, what it was in the beginning: the Body of Christ on earth.

In Acts 1:20, when the apostles discern the need to replace Judas, Peter refers to the Psalms and says, *"Let another take his office."* The Greek word translated as "office" is ἐπισκοπή (episkopē), from which we derive the word *episcopal*—meaning bishop. This was not just about maintaining twelve seats around a symbolic table. It was about preserving the divinely appointed leadership of the Church. Matthias is not just a placeholder; he is a successor. And with that succession, the pattern is established.

The Structure That Held

As the Church began to grow, she did not simply improvise leadership out of practicality—she followed the pattern Christ had initiated. We see the apostles taking deliberate action not only to preach and baptize, but to appoint leaders in every community they established.

Paul and Barnabas, on their missionary journeys, *"appointed elders [πρεσβυτέρους, presbyterous] for them in every church"* (Acts 14:23).

This Greek word—*presbyteros*—gives us the root for what we now call the priesthood. It literally means "elder," but it is clear from context that this was not a generic label for respected men in the community. These were spiritual shepherds, entrusted with teaching, leading, and sacramental responsibility.

Alongside *presbyteroi*, we find *episkopoi*—translated as "overseers" or "bishops." Paul refers to them directly in Philippians 1:1, when he writes, *"To all the saints in Christ Jesus who are at Philippi, with the bishops [ἐπίσκοποι, episkopoi] and deacons [διάκονοι, diakonoi]..."* Notice how clearly the structure emerges: the faithful, the bishops, and the deacons—a Church already showing threefold leadership rooted in divine mission, not personal preference.

Later, Paul instructs Titus, *"This is why I left you in Crete... that you might appoint presbyters in every town"* (Titus 1:5). Then, just a few verses later, he refers to the role as that of a bishop (*episkopos*), showing that these terms—though sometimes used interchangeably—were already forming into the distinct roles we see today in Catholic teaching: bishop, priest, and deacon.

Not Just a Human Arrangement

Some argue that this structure was a human invention—an efficient way to organize a growing movement. But that doesn't hold up to Scripture. If Christ entrusted His authority to the apostles, and if that authority was passed on deliberately to others through prayer and the laying on of hands (cf. 2 Tim 1:6, Acts 13:3), then we are not looking at something *optional*. We are looking at the very means by which Christ chose to remain present in His Church.

Paul doesn't simply "suggest" these structures. He commands them. He tells Timothy and Titus to appoint leaders who are morally sound, doctrinally firm, and worthy of imitation—not because it's helpful, but because it is essential. The Church is not a loose association of independent believers. It is a body, with members, and that body must have order.

And it is not a coincidence that this order reflects heaven.

A Voice from the Early Church

If there were ever a moment to lean in and ask, "What did the earliest Christians believe?"—this is it. The Book of Acts lays the foundation, but the Church Fathers—the direct disciples of the apostles—build upon it. And one voice stands out with piercing clarity: Ignatius of Antioch.

Writing around A.D. 107 on his way to martyrdom in Rome, Ignatius—who tradition holds was a disciple of the apostle John—left behind seven letters. In them, he does not speculate about Church structure or suggest a more efficient model. He assumes the model already exists and exhorts the faithful to remain loyal to it. In his *Letter to the Smyrnaeans*, he writes:

> *"Wherever the bishop appears, there let the people be; just as wherever Jesus Christ is, there is the Catholic Church."*

This is the first known use of the phrase *Catholic Church* in written form. And Ignatius uses it to describe the one visible, sacramentally united Church under apostolic leadership, which he understood as being inseparable from Christ Himself. In his letters, he clearly distinguishes between:

• The bishop (*episkopos*) as the successor of the apostles,

• The presbyters as the priestly collaborators of the bishop,

• And the deacons, who serve the Church with sacramental and charitable roles.

Ignatius warns that no Eucharist is valid apart from the bishop or one to whom the bishop has entrusted it. No baptism or marriage should take place without his oversight. Why? Because without apostolic succession, the community becomes detached from the Body of Christ, and what remains is no longer the Church, but a shadow of it.

Protecting the Truth Through Time

Christ promised to remain with His Church. But how would that Church recognize true teaching from false? How would it guard the deposit of faith as it faced heresies, persecutions, and cultural shifts?

The answer is apostolic succession. Paul writes to Timothy:

"Guard the truth that has been entrusted to you by the Holy Spirit who dwells within us" (2 Tim 1:14).

"What you have heard from me before many witnesses entrust to faithful men who will be able to teach others also" (2 Tim 2:2).

That is four generations of transmission in just one passage:

1 Paul,

2 Timothy,

3 Faithful men,

4 Those they will teach.

This isn't accidental. This is succession. And it doesn't depend on charisma or personal conviction. It depends on ordination, unity, and the apostolic office that Christ Himself established.

We often hear the question: *"Why can't I just read the Bible and follow Jesus?"*

You can. But how do you know what the Bible means? Who determined which books belonged in it? Who preserved it, copied it, protected it? Who interpreted it when conflicts arose? And who still has the authority to declare what is essential to the faith?

The answer, again and again, is the Catholic Church—not because Catholics are more intelligent or spiritually superior, but because the Church has been divinely protected by Christ to serve as a pillar and bulwark of truth (cf. 1 Tim 3:15). It is not the book that safeguards the Church. It is the Church that safeguarded the book.

A Living Chain

Every bishop in the Catholic Church today was ordained by another bishop, who was ordained by another, who was ordained by another—reaching back, one link at a time, to the apostles. This isn't romantic storytelling. It is verifiable history. There are even historical lineages—some traced from Peter to Linus to Cletus to Clement—with corresponding evidence from Roman and Eastern records alike.

This is not about human control. It's about divine continuity.

To believe that the Church was real in Acts, but is now a scattered imitation built by good intentions, is to believe in a Christ who only intended to accompany His people for a little while—and then abandoned them. But the Catholic faith says otherwise.

It says: He is still here.

Through Word. Through Sacrament. Through the hands and hearts of the successors He ordained.

The Church Is Not a Quiz

It is a strange modern idea that in order to belong to a Church, we must first understand and agree with everything it teaches—*perfectly*.

And if we don't? Well, then it's time to break away and start over. Time to form a new church. A new community. A new "movement of the Spirit."

But is that how the apostles lived?

Read the Gospels closely, and you will find men who followed Jesus with their hearts long before they understood everything with their minds. When He spoke of eating His flesh and drinking His blood, many walked away. But Peter said, *"Lord, to whom shall we go? You have the words of eternal life"* (John 6:68). Not, "I understand," but "I trust You."

Faith means walking forward even when all the pieces haven't clicked into place. The apostles didn't grasp the full meaning of Christ's words while He was alive. They argued. They misunderstood. At times, they even resisted Him. But they stayed. They obeyed. And their belief deepened into understanding over time, not in a single flash of insight.

So why do so many modern Christians insist that unless every doctrine is easy to understand, every teaching emotionally agreeable, and every answer intellectually satisfying from the outset, the Church must be wrong—or worse, replaced?

The truth is, we don't need a Church that simply mirrors our preferences or offers digestible answers. We need a Church that teaches with divine authority, even when it stretches us beyond comfort. We need a Church that invites surrender, not just agreement.

That's why today, we see countless former Protestants entering the Catholic Church—not because every question has been answered to their satisfaction, but because something deeper has stirred. A conviction. A recognition. A quiet voice in the soul that says, *"This is true."* And then, *"This is home."*

That voice doesn't come from clever arguments or well-polished theology. It comes from the Holy Spirit.

And the Spirit does not sow confusion. Yet what do we see when every individual becomes their own final authority? Tens of thousands of denominations. Disagreements over baptism, marriage, salvation, worship, morality, and more—all among Christians who claim Scripture alone as their rule of faith.

One book. One Lord. Thousands of conflicting interpretations.

The apostles didn't build a structure of personal interpretation and private opinion. They built a Church. With unity. With authority. With succession. And Christ said the gates of hell would not prevail against it.

That Church is still here. Not because we've figured out every mystery, but because we've received the fullness of truth handed down through the apostles. Not because we've personally solved every theological question, but because we trust the voice of Christ speaking through His Church.

It is not about blind belief or settling for partial truth. It is about recognizing the divine authority of a Church that does not speak on its own, but guards what she has received. The same Church that spoke with authority in Acts still speaks today. And it speaks not because of human wisdom, but because of the Holy Spirit who remains with her always.

And through it all, the words of Christ still echo at the foundation: 'You are Peter, and on this rock I will build my Church.' The Church in Acts is not something new. It is the unfolding of a promise made on the road to Caesarea Philippi.

Voices Across the Ages

The truth of the Church is not guarded by emotion or tradition alone—it is echoed across centuries by those who have studied her deeply, loved her honestly, and at times even questioned her from the outside. Whether in the passionate defense of the Church Fathers, the clarity of Catholic theologians, or the reluctant admiration of Protestant historians, the pattern is visible: the Church that Christ founded in Acts is not lost. She has lived, taught, and continued, from generation to generation.

St. Irenaeus of Lyons, writing around A.D. 180, was one of the earliest defenders of apostolic succession. Confronting the rise of heresies in his day, he made this plain:

"It is within the power of all... to contemplate clearly the tradition of the apostles manifested throughout the whole world; and we are in a position to enumerate those who were instituted bishops by the apostles and their successors to our own times."

—*Against Heresies*, III.3.1

More than a millennium later, and outside the Catholic fold, J. N. D. Kelly, a respected Anglican scholar of early Christian doctrine, came to the same conclusion:

"Everywhere in the early Church the bishop is the focal point of unity. The Church was thought of as gathered around the bishop. His authority was regarded as derived from the apostles, and ultimately from Christ."

—*Early Christian Doctrines*, p. 205

Catholic theologian Scott Hahn, a former Presbyterian minister and convert, sees in apostolic succession not a chain of power, but a chain of fidelity:

"Apostolic succession is not a chain of command, but a chain of custody—for truth. The bishops are not spiritual monarchs, but guardians of the deposit of faith."

—*Many Are Called: Rediscovering the Glory of the Priesthood*, p. 87

From the Orthodox tradition, Fr. Georges Florovsky affirms that apostolic continuity is not just a Catholic claim—it is central to the very nature of the Church:

"The Church is neither an organization nor a society, but a Divine institution and organism—the very Body of Christ. Apostolic succession is the very form of this organic unity and continuity."

—*The Catholicity of the Church* (1934)

And finally, Pope Benedict XVI, a towering mind and gentle shepherd of the modern Church, offers this simple and profound insight:

"The Church is not ours, but His. We do not make it; we are called into it. It is in the Church, through her continuity, that we encounter the living Christ."

—*Called to Communion*, p. 143

Their words are not random endorsements. They are witnesses to what the heart often knows before the mind understands: that the Church of Acts is not a relic—it is a reality. Still with us. Still teaching. Still proclaiming the Gospel. Still raising up successors. Still offering the sacraments that bring us home.

Because Christ did not build His Church for one moment in history.

He built it for every soul, in every age—including ours.

Chapter 6

The Council of Jerusalem: A Church that Decides

Every family has disagreements. Even those who love one another and share the same core values will find themselves, from time to time, at odds over difficult questions. The Church is no different. From the very beginning, the Christian community faced real and sometimes heated disputes. But what made the Church different—what still makes her different—is how those disputes are resolved.

Acts 15 presents us with one of the earliest and most important challenges in the history of Christianity: the question of whether Gentile converts must follow the Mosaic Law, including circumcision, in order to be saved. It was not a minor disagreement. It went to the very heart of salvation, covenant, and identity. Some believers, described as coming from the Pharisee party, insisted that unless Gentiles were circumcised according to the Law of Moses, they could not be saved.

The dispute might have led to a schism. Two camps. Two gospels. Two incompatible theological paths. But instead, what we see is a gathering—a council. The apostles and elders meet in Jerusalem not to brainstorm or take a poll, but to seek the guidance of the Holy Spirit and come to a binding decision. And presiding over this moment, as the visible center of unity, is Peter.

He listens. He allows debate. He lets others speak. But when he stands and speaks, the room quiets. *"Brothers, you know that in the early days God made a choice among you, that by my mouth the Gentiles should hear the word of the gospel and believe"* (Acts 15:7). Peter does not claim new revelation. He appeals to what God has already done—through him. And when he concludes, *"we believe that we shall be saved through the grace of the Lord Jesus, just as they will"* (Acts 15:11), the matter is no longer open.

James, the bishop of Jerusalem, speaks next, affirming Peter's words and suggesting pastoral provisions. But he does not override Peter. He affirms. The Church, united, issues its decision not with suggestion, but with authority: *"It has seemed good to the Holy Spirit and to us..."* (Acts 15:28).

This moment is pivotal. It is the first ecumenical council, foreshadowing all those that would follow—from Nicaea to Trent to Vatican II. And it is here that we see clearly: the Church does not survive by consensus. She does not scatter into factions. She does not choose truth by majority vote. She discerns in communion, and she speaks with authority.

And through it all, Peter's voice stands at the center. The one who was told, *"You are Peter,"* now shepherds the Church through conflict—not as a tyrant, but as the one Christ appointed to confirm the brethren (cf. Luke 22:32).

Who Really Led the Council?

Some readers of Acts 15 are quick to suggest that James—not Peter—was the true leader of the early Church. After all, James speaks last. He proposes the written decision. His voice appears to carry weight.

But a closer look at the passage reveals something different—something crucial.

Yes, James is the bishop of Jerusalem. That alone gives him a key role in hosting the council and issuing the pastoral guidelines that would follow. But James does not decide the doctrine. Peter does.

It is Peter who rises and speaks after the debate. And it is Peter who declares, not suggests, that *"we believe that we shall be saved through the grace of the Lord Jesus, just as they will."* This is not a theological reflection. It is a doctrinal conclusion. And the text makes it clear: *"And all the assembly kept silence"* (Acts 15:12).

Peter ends the debate. James affirms the conclusion. He offers pastoral language and practical implementation—proposing which parts of Mosaic custom should be respected to maintain peace between Jewish and Gentile Christians. But his speech stands on the foundation of Peter's decision.

This is exactly the pattern we would expect if Peter were the visible head of the Church. His role is not to dominate the conversation, but to settle it. Just as Jesus spoke final words in parables and confrontations that left His opponents silent, Peter now speaks with clarity that leaves the council in agreement.

If James had contradicted Peter—if he had proposed a different theological outcome—we would see chaos. But there is no contradiction. There is no rewording of doctrine. There is only harmony. And that harmony exists because the voice of Peter has spoken.

This is not incidental. It is not interpretive sleight of hand. It is a visible manifestation of what Christ intended when He said, *"You are Peter... and I will give you the keys."* It is also the living fulfillment of Christ's words in Luke 22:32, *"I have prayed for you, that your faith may not fail; and when you have turned again, strengthen your brethren."*

This is what Peter is doing in Acts 15: strengthening his brethren, not with personality or politics, but with the authority given him by Christ.

One Voice, Many Brothers

What we witness at the Council of Jerusalem is not a dictatorship—it is a family. And like any family, there are different roles. Different personalities. Different charisms. Peter speaks with authority, but not in isolation. He listens first. He allows the debate to unfold. He discerns. Then, when the moment comes, he speaks not to dominate, but to confirm.

James, in his pastoral wisdom, reinforces Peter's doctrinal decision and offers a path for peaceful implementation. Paul and Barnabas contribute through testimony. The whole assembly participates in the discernment. And when the Church moves forward, it does so not because Peter demanded it, but because the Holy Spirit, through Peter, made the truth clear.

This moment is a powerful reminder that the Church needs all her parts. She needs the visible head—but also the body. She needs the clarity of authority—but also the depth of tradition, experience, and wisdom that comes from the communion of bishops.

Here, we see a model that continues into our own day—and which still calls for unity between East and West. The Orthodox Churches, in their fidelity to the early Fathers, liturgical richness, and sacramental depth, carry treasures that the Catholic Church recognizes and esteems. Their contribution to the early councils was not marginal—it was foundational. Their role in forming doctrine, preserving apostolic liturgy, and guiding the faithful is woven into the fabric of Christianity itself.

And yet, the visible unity of the Church—then and now—depends on the one who has been given the keys. Not because he is infallible on his own. Not because his personality is superior. But because, as Christ promised, the Holy Spirit would guide him in safeguarding the faith (cf. John 14:26; Luke 22:32).

Peter could be influenced. He could learn from others. He could be corrected, as Paul later would do—not in doctrine, but in practice. But he could not lead the Church into error, because he was not leading alone. The Spirit was guiding him, and the brethren were walking with him.

This is not a flaw. It is the genius of the Church: a divinely established office, protected by the Holy Spirit, supported by a communion of bishops, entrusted with the care of souls.

The Church does not thrive by force. She thrives by fidelity—fidelity to Christ, to the apostles, to the faith handed down, and to one another. East and West. Clergy and laity. Bishop and brother. This is not competition—it is communion.

And it all began with a council. With a disagreement. With a moment that could have divided the early Church—but didn't. Why?

Because Peter stood up, the apostles stood together, and the Holy Spirit spoke through them.

A Blueprint for Unity, A Warning of Division

What emerged from the Council of Jerusalem was more than a doctrinal ruling. It was a blueprint for the Church's future—how to address questions, how to hold tensions together, and how to discern the voice of the Holy Spirit amid human limitation.

That pattern—gathering in council, listening to the bishops in communion with Peter, and then speaking with one voice—became the lifeblood of the Church's unity. Whether in Nicaea, Chalcedon, or Constantinople, the model held: the Church did not innovate her faith; she clarified and defended it. The Spirit did not speak through division, but through discernment, prayer, and communion.

But as history would soon show, a blueprint can be misused. What God had given as a path for unity would become, in the hands of the proud and the powerful, a battleground. As the Church expanded across cultures, languages, and political empires, tensions would rise, and egos would clash. What was once familial charity began to turn into suspicion. Disagreements became hardened positions. And eventually, wounds turned into walls.

It would not happen overnight. And it would not be a rejection of Christ. But it would mark a painful rupture in the visible Body of Christ—a moment that has echoed through a thousand years of separation.

The Church still had her structure. She still had the sacraments, the apostolic faith, the councils, the bishop of Rome. But communion between East and West—between brothers—would be deeply wounded.

And so, we turn now from the pattern Christ gave, to the fracture history delivered—not to dwell in division, but to better understand the path to healing.

Chapter 7

The Catholic Mission Continues

The Shepherd's Final Word

Peter knew he would die.

Not just because Christ had told him (cf. John 21:18), but because the world was growing darker—and the cost of leadership in the name of Jesus was rising.

In his final letter, written from Rome, Peter exhorted the Church not to waver. He warned of false teachers, of prideful ambition, of moral decay. But more than anything, he pointed to hope:

> *"I think it right, as long as I am in this body, to arouse you by way of reminder... so that after my departure you may be able at any time to recall these things."*
>
> *(2 Peter 1:13–15)*

In 1 Peter 5:13, he sends greetings from "Babylon"—a symbolic name used by early Christians to refer to Rome, especially during times of persecution. Just as ancient Babylon had once been a place of exile and suffering for the Jewish people, Rome had become the epicenter of imperial power and hostility toward the Christian faith. This symbolic language was both pastoral and protective, shielding believers from unnecessary exposure during dangerous times.

Peter's presence and martyrdom in Rome are not matters of speculation—they are rooted in the earliest records of the Church. St. Clement of Rome (writing in the first century), St. Ignatius of Antioch, St. Irenaeus, Tertullian, and the historian Eusebius of Caesarea all affirm that Peter exercised his apostolic ministry in Rome and was martyred there under Emperor Nero, likely between A.D. 64 and 68. Tradition holds that he was crucified upside down, at his own request, declaring that he was unworthy to die in the same manner as Christ.

His tomb beneath what is now St. Peter's Basilica continues to serve as a physical and spiritual witness to his leadership, sacrifice, and enduring role in the life of the Church.

And yet... the Church did not die with him.

The mission did not end at the crossbeam of Peter's martyrdom. It pressed on. With the successors he and the other apostles had appointed. With the Scriptures beginning to take shape. With the sacraments still celebrated and the Gospel still preached. The Church did not scatter. She organized. She remembered. And she remained.

She did not define herself by a name but by a mission.

But that mission? It was already unmistakably Catholic.

In A.D. 107, St. Ignatius of Antioch, writing on his way to martyrdom, would call the Church by the name it had already come to live:

Catholic—universal, unified, apostolic, and holy.

Her bishops were in place. Her Eucharist was sacred. Her heart was beating strong.

Before the wound of division, the Church was one.

The Christ-appointed *Shepherd* had died. But the sheepfold endured.

A Mission with a Memory

The death of Peter was not the end of anything. It was, in many ways, a beginning. The Church he helped lead was not dependent on one man's life, but on the foundation Christ had laid through the apostles—and on the promise of the Holy Spirit, who would remain with them always (cf. John 14:16).

The apostles had passed on more than teachings. They had ordained bishops to continue their work. They had formed communities, not around themselves, but around the breaking of the bread, the preaching of the Word, and the safeguarding of truth. This wasn't disorganized spiritual inspiration—it was the bones and breath of a living Body.

The bishop of Rome had already emerged as a central point of reference and unity. When disputes arose in places like Corinth, the local churches turned to Rome for help—not because of military strength or political power, but because Rome had received both Peter and Paul, had endured persecution, and had shown faithful witness in the heart of the empire.

The letters of Clement of Rome, written near the end of the first century, reflect this early voice of leadership. Clement appeals for peace, unity, and the maintenance of apostolic order. And he does so not as a meddler, but as a shepherd concerned with the health of the whole flock.

St. Ignatius of Antioch, writing just a few years later on his way to martyrdom, speaks of the Roman Church with unmistakable reverence, calling it the one that "presides in love." This was not flattery. It was recognition. The early Church understood that unity was not an abstract ideal—it had a form, and a center.

By the early second century, the word "Catholic" was already in use—not as a rebranding or institutional label, but as a description of the Church's reality. It was universal, drawing all people to Christ. It was orthodox, safeguarding the truth handed down from the apostles. And it was visible, structured, and sacramental.

This is what made the mission effective. This is why, as the apostles died, the Church did not splinter. The blueprint was already in place.

And when the time came for deeper questions to arise—questions about the nature of Christ, about heresies and confusion, about Scripture and creeds—it was this apostolic structure that allowed the Church to gather, to pray, and to decide.

The blueprint didn't die with Peter. It went to work.

The Successors Step Forward

It is a strange and holy thing to become the first man to sit in Peter's chair.

Linus likely never thought of it that way. Chairs were for elders, not monuments. There was no gold, no ornate symbols. Just a heavy weight of duty and an unspoken understanding: Christ had chosen Peter… and Peter had chosen him.

We do not have many words from Linus. But we have his name—written by Paul in a passing line of 2 Timothy, like a nod to a brother known well enough to need no explanation. Tradition, confirmed by Irenaeus and Eusebius, tells us that Peter ordained Linus, and that he succeeded Peter as the bishop of Rome.

And what kind of Church did Linus inherit?

One bruised and beautiful. The great apostles were being hunted down. Nero's shadow still hung over the city like smoke. Converts were rising, but so were false teachers. Rome was massive, diverse, disoriented. And yet somehow, the community of believers held together. It wasn't just preaching or charisma—it was apostolic authority, passed on, guarded, and lived out.

Linus led without applause. He would have celebrated the Eucharist in secret, appointed priests in quiet homes, and encouraged the faithful who walked every day with the risk of martyrdom. His job was not to reinvent, but to remember. He carried Peter's voice in his bones.

After Linus came Anacletus, and then Clement—each chosen not through election by popularity, but through the mind of the Church led by the Holy Spirit. By the time Clement became bishop, the role of Rome was becoming clearer to the wider Christian world.

When a serious division broke out in the Church of Corinth—some younger members rising up against elders—Clement of Rome stepped in. He didn't do it by force. He did it with fatherly concern. His letter, known to us today as *1 Clement*, is one of the earliest Christian writings outside the New Testament. And it speaks volumes.

He doesn't say, "I'm the boss." He says, "Let us return to the tradition we received." He speaks of the apostles appointing bishops, and of bishops handing on their office—not as inventors of doctrine, but as guardians of something sacred. What's remarkable is that Clement writes with authority to a distant church, even while the Apostle John was still alive. And the Corinthians listened.

The early Church saw Rome not just as another city, but as a place where the fullness of apostolic witness had taken root. Both Peter and Paul had been martyred there. The soil was soaked with their blood. The bishop of Rome wasn't a political figure—he was a shepherd in the line of Peter, whose role was to maintain unity, uphold truth, and settle disputes when needed.

These early successors were not flawless men. They were not mythic figures of legend. They were likely tired, burdened, courageous, and —at times—terrified. But they were faithful. And they were part of a Church that was alive, organic, and deeply ordered.

Apostolic succession was not a theory. It was embodied in men who had to make hard decisions in dangerous times. And it was their presence that gave the Church something the outside world did not understand: continuity.

The death of Peter had not ended the Church. It had lit a fire that could not be put out.

Into the Heart of the Empire

If there had been a safer place to plant the Church, Peter didn't choose it.

Rome was no holy city. It was a pagan empire swollen with idols, military conquest, and the illusion of invincibility. But Peter went anyway. So did Paul. The Church's two great apostles, different in personality but united in mission, both made their final stand in the capital of the empire.

To an outsider, it might have seemed foolish. Why would Peter go to Rome, the very city most likely to crush him? Why lead the Church from its most dangerous corner?

Because Rome was the center of the world. And Peter's mission, entrusted to him by Christ, was not local—it was universal. Rome was not simply where power was concentrated; it was where people from every corner of the empire came and went. To bring the Gospel to Rome was to set a match to the crossroads of civilization.

But more than that, Peter knew what lay ahead. Jesus had told him plainly: *"When you are old, you will stretch out your hands, and another will dress you and carry you where you do not want to go."* (John 21:18)

Peter was going to Rome to die. But his death would not be defeat. It would be testimony. Rome would become the new Jerusalem—not in replacement, but in mission. The city that once stood as Babylon, the seat of worldly glory, would be reclaimed and reoriented by apostolic witness.

In his first epistle, Peter subtly signals his location by closing with the line, *"She who is at Babylon, who is likewise chosen, sends you greetings."* (1 Peter 5:13) Babylon was a code word for Rome. It carried weight: a history of oppression, confusion, and paganism. But Peter does not curse it—he blesses it. The new Church is rising within the heart of the old empire. He's not hiding. He's planting.

When the time came, Peter was arrested and, according to tradition, crucified upside down—by his own request, feeling unworthy to die as his Lord had. His death was not the end of the papacy but its cornerstone. And his grave, somewhere beneath the modern basilica in Vatican City, remains a silent yet bold declaration: the rock is still here.

From this moment on, Rome became the city of apostolic memory. Not because Peter sought fame or control, but because the Church needed an anchor. Something rooted. Someone who had heard the Lord, seen the risen Christ, and passed on the mission through successors who were willing to die rather than distort what had been given.

The Church's Identity Clarified

The Church had lost her earthly shepherd, but not her voice.

Peter's death in Rome was not the silencing of the Gospel—it was its amplification. His martyrdom confirmed what had already been written in his letters: *"The God of all grace, who has called you to his eternal glory in Christ, will himself restore, establish, and strengthen you."* (1 Peter 5:10, RSVCE)

And this is what began to happen. The infant Church, forged in blood and grounded in apostolic witness, now stood on the shoulders of Peter's successors. Rome remained the anchor, not because of its imperial status, but because it held the bones of the one Christ called the Rock. The mission continued—not under a new authority, but under the same Spirit who guided the apostles from the beginning.

By the early second century, this identity was becoming clearer. The Church did not name herself to compete with others. She called herself *Catholic* because she was universal in scope, united in doctrine, and sent forth to all peoples. The name simply arose to describe what she already was.

In A.D. 107, St. Ignatius of Antioch, on his way to martyrdom in Rome, wrote in his letter to the Smyrnaeans:

"Wherever Jesus Christ is, there is the Catholic Church."

This was not a branding strategy. It was a description of reality. The Church was not a series of disconnected congregations improvising doctrine. She was one, gathered around her bishops, and especially around the bishop who sat in the place of Peter.

This doesn't mean the Church's title was more important than her mission. On the contrary, her mission gave rise to her name. She was Catholic in heart and practice before she was Catholic in vocabulary.

And that mission—universal, unifying, evangelical—continued. The successors of Peter—Linus, Anacletus, and Clement—led not as monarchs, but as stewards. There was no ambition in being pope in the early centuries—only danger. But there was also purpose: to guard what had been received, and to shepherd the Church in unity and truth.

It's worth noting that the word *Pope* was not yet the common title in these earliest years. It would gradually come into use, derived from the simple, familial word *papa*—"father." It was never meant to elevate a man as divine, but to reflect his role as a spiritual father in the Church. Just as Paul called himself a spiritual father to the communities he guided (cf. 1 Corinthians 4:15), so too did this affectionate title emerge for the one tasked with preserving unity among the faithful.

The pope is not a rival to God, nor a replacement for Christ, but a servant of the servants of God. His office is not about power, but protection. His commission is not self-declared, but inherited from the words of Christ to Peter: *"Feed my sheep."*

For those who may feel uneasy about this title, it's important to remember: the name came later, but the role was present from the beginning. The man who served as Peter's successor did not invent the mission—he simply carried it forward. In the same way that the Church was Catholic in heart before it was Catholic in name, so too was the Petrine ministry at work before the word *pope* was ever spoken aloud.

The blueprint left by Acts was now coming to life. The apostles had set it in motion, and the post-apostolic Church began to follow it. There were bishops in every city, presbyters to preach and teach, and deacons to serve. The structure was taking shape, not as an invention of man, but as the unfolding of divine intention.

And as the Church spread, she would soon need something more formal: councils to clarify doctrine, correct errors, and confirm unity.

But even these councils would not stand above the apostles. They would only echo the voice of the One who founded the Church—not on an idea, but on a man named Peter, whose witness now sanctified the very soil of Rome.

Chapter 8

Guardians of the Deposit: Councils and Clarity

The Church was alive and growing.

Though the apostles had passed, their teaching had not. It lived in the liturgies, the letters, the creeds whispered in homes, and the Eucharist celebrated in secret. The bishops, ordained in apostolic succession, now bore the responsibility of protecting this sacred inheritance—the *deposit of faith*.

But with growth came challenge. And with challenge came the need for clarity.

Not everything that claimed to be Christian was faithful to the teaching of Christ. Heresies emerged—some subtle, others bold. Some denied Christ's divinity. Others denied His humanity. And in a world without printing presses, digital archives, or instant messaging, how could the Church stay united?

The answer had already been given in Acts 15: gather the Church's shepherds, pray, debate, and decide under the guidance of the Holy Spirit.

The blueprint of the Council of Jerusalem had not been forgotten. It was time for the bishops to come together once more—not in Jerusalem, but in a city called Nicaea.

A Council Like No Other

The First Council of Nicaea was unlike anything the Church had seen since the apostles.

Over 300 bishops came, traveling from as far as Spain, Egypt, and Persia. Many still bore the scars of persecution—blinded eyes, missing limbs, twisted hands. These were men who had suffered for Christ. Now they came to stand for Him once more.

They gathered not to vote on opinions but to discern and define what the Church had always believed. Their goal was not to create a new doctrine, but to guard the one handed down from the apostles.

At the heart of the council stood a young deacon named Athanasius, assistant to the bishop of Alexandria. Though not yet a bishop himself, Athanasius would become the great defender of the Incarnation. It was he who insisted: Christ is *homoousios* with the Father—of the same substance, not merely like Him.

This word, *homoousios*, became the theological line in the sand. It would make its way into the creed the bishops composed, which we still profess today at Mass:

> "God from God, Light from Light,
> true God from true God,
> begotten, not made,
> consubstantial with the Father."

Arius was condemned. His teachings were declared heretical. And for the first time, the universal Church had spoken as one, not by inventing truth, but by clarifying it.

The Church had learned something vital: when the truth is challenged, unity must be defended not by retreat, but by communion. Not in isolation, but in council.

The Role of Rome: Unity through Confirmation

Though the Council of Nicaea was called in the East and presided over by Eastern bishops, it was not independent of Rome. In fact, the Pope—St. Sylvester I—did not attend in person due to age and distance, but he sent two legates as official representatives. These men carried the voice and judgment of the bishop of Rome.

This was not unusual. The East often convened councils in its own territory, closer to the heart of the empire. But it was understood, both implicitly and eventually explicitly, that for a council to be truly ecumenical—that is, *universal and binding* on the whole Church—it must be confirmed by the Pope.

Not because the pope was a tyrant. But because he was the *servant of unity*.

The early Church Fathers said it clearly:

"Rome has spoken; the matter is settled."

— St. Augustine, c. 417 A.D., reflecting on Pope Innocent I's decision regarding the Pelagian controversy

"You cannot appeal to a council against the bishop of Rome."

— St. Jerome, in his letters regarding disputes over authority

The Pope was seen not as a distant overlord but as the *center of gravity*—a shepherd who held the Church together when the storms of division threatened to pull it apart.

This did not mean Rome ruled alone. The Eastern bishops were powerful voices. Men like Athanasius, Basil the Great, Gregory of

Nazianzus, and John Chrysostom were not puppets of Rome, nor were they marginalized. They were champions of orthodoxy who *worked with* the bishop of Rome, not against him.

In fact, the Church functioned best in these early centuries when the East and West worked together—councils clarifying truth, popes confirming their decrees, and bishops returning home with unity and renewed strength for the people.

This was the blueprint established at Nicaea. And it would be followed for the next six ecumenical councils, each one called to address false teachings and preserve the apostolic faith.

From Clarifying Doctrine to Guarding Communion

The early centuries of the Church showed that even as her flock spread into distant lands, the need for communion remained essential. Councils had offered clarity, but they also revealed something else: the deep dependence the bishops had on one another—especially between East and West. The churches in Alexandria, Antioch, Jerusalem, and Constantinople were vibrant and intellectually rich. Their theologians were among the greatest minds in Christian history. But it was still Rome that the early Church looked to for confirmation, especially when clarity of doctrine needed to be sealed with unity.

Yet even as the Church grew in grace and understanding, so too did tension. Language barriers between Latin and Greek, political divisions between the Eastern and Western empires, and differing liturgical expressions all played a part. Theological disagreements occasionally flared, but none more significant than a single phrase that, though meant to defend the divinity of Christ, would become a symbol of fracture: *filioque*.

In Latin, *filioque* means "and the Son." It was a phrase inserted into the Nicene Creed in the Western Church, affirming that the Holy

Spirit "proceeds from the Father *and the Son*." This addition, intended to combat heresy in the West, was not debated or agreed upon by the Eastern bishops. And to the East, this change—made unilaterally—felt like a breach of ecclesial trust.

At the heart of the issue was not simply a theological disagreement, but a question of authority. Could one part of the Church, even with noble intentions, adjust a creed formed in council without universal agreement?

The tension simmered for centuries, occasionally boiling over in acts of misunderstanding, pride, and failed diplomacy. Eventually, in 1054, the fragile bond between East and West would rupture. The Great Schism was not born overnight. It was the result of accumulated wounds—some theological, some cultural, many personal. But the result was undeniable: two lungs of the same Body were no longer breathing in sync.

Still, it must be said—the Church did not become two Churches. She became a wounded family. The Orthodox Church did not reject the Sacraments, the Eucharist, the Virgin Birth, the apostolic succession, or the authority of bishops. What fractured was not the core deposit of faith, but the communion that once held it in visible unity. And even in separation, both East and West continued to defend the truth of the Gospel, each preserving what they had received.

A Church of Complementary Strengths

As the first centuries of the Church unfolded, the mystery of unity was not rooted in uniformity—but in complementarity. The Church breathed with both lungs—East and West—not as opposing poles of theology or hierarchy, but as expressions of one shared faith. The theological brilliance of the East and the pastoral, juridical, and missionary clarity of the West were not in competition. They were collaborative. Co-responsible. Co-essential.

The councils of the Church did not exist to discover new doctrines or force agreement. They were spiritual, reasoned responses to crisis. Heresies had emerged—not as outside attacks—but from within the body, from those confused or misled. In each case, the bishops gathered in council to wrestle with Scripture, tradition, and the lived faith of the people of God. But once their work was done, it was the Bishop of Rome who confirmed their conclusions—not to assert personal power, but to preserve the apostolic deposit of faith.

The West was not the theological undercard. The Church in Rome, from the earliest generations, had produced voices of extraordinary weight: St. Clement I, whose letter to the Corinthians was so widely respected it was sometimes read in churches alongside Scripture; St. Leo the Great, whose *Tome* helped shape the Council of Chalcedon's declaration on Christ's two natures; St. Augustine, whose writings would form the theological backbone of Western Christianity for over a millennium.

And then, when emperors and eastern pressure supported heresy, it was often the Bishop of Rome who stood firm, even at great cost. The martyrdom of Pope Martin I, who condemned Monothelitism at the Lateran Council of 649 and was kidnapped by order of Emperor Constans II, remains a shining witness to the courage and conviction of the papacy in upholding the truth, even when it was politically dangerous to do so.

In this way, Rome's leadership was not arbitrary, nor did it develop in a vacuum. It was seen as a source of strength, of unity, and of continuity—not just for the West, but for the whole Church. As the bishops of Chalcedon famously declared in A.D. 451, upon hearing Pope Leo's letter: *"Peter has spoken through Leo."*

This is the heart of Catholic unity: not domination, but confirmation. Not suppression of voice, but preservation of truth. Not an isolated dictatorship, but the Church acting as one, in which Peter's successor is tasked with strengthening his brothers (cf. Luke 22:32).

A Wound No Longer Avoidable

Long before a single word was added to the Nicene Creed, the Church had already begun to feel the pressure of a growing divide.

It wasn't one moment or one issue. It was centuries of slow drift.

The East and West had developed along different cultural lines—Greek and Latin, Byzantine and Roman. Political power had shifted. Emperors came and went. Language, liturgy, and leadership styles shaped how Christians lived and guided their communities. The Bishop of Rome—always seen as holding a unique and unifying role—was now being viewed by some with increasing suspicion, especially as the West exercised that role more definitively.

Into that already fragile space came the filioque.

What began as a regional clarification—affirming that the Holy Spirit proceeds not only from the Father but also from the Son—eventually made its way into the Western version of the Nicene Creed. But rather than revisit the issue together in council, as had been the custom, the West adopted the phrase unilaterally in response to local heresies.

This sparked deep concern in the East. Not simply because of theological nuance, but because the conciliar method—*how* decisions had been made together—seemed to have been bypassed.

Still, it would be inaccurate to say that either side "walked away." This wasn't a protest, or a reformation, or a revolution. No one abandoned the Church. There was no official announcement of departure. Instead, there was a tragic rupture in communion—like a family that no longer speaks, no longer listens, no longer sits together at the same table.

The filioque was not the sole cause of the schism, but it revealed how fragile the bond had become. What had once been a shared breath between East and West began to wheeze in disharmony. The Church wasn't destroyed, but deeply wounded.

And yet, even then, the identity of the Church did not dissolve.

The mission continued. The sacraments endured. Apostolic succession remained intact. The papacy did not become something new; it remained the Office of Peter, now carrying its burden without the full support of its Eastern brethren.

This was not the unraveling of what Christ established. It was the sorrowful silence between siblings. A Church still one in origin, but divided in expression.

And so, the stage was set.

Chapter 9

Trials, Truth, and the Call for Unity

The early Church was not born in peace and prosperity—it was born into chaos.

This was an age of persecution, where Christians were hunted, arrested, and killed for their faith. It was also a time of shifting political borders, fragile alliances, and empires that rose and fell with breathtaking speed. The Roman Empire, though expansive, was often unstable, and its emperors sometimes wielded immense influence over religious life—sometimes in favor of the Church, but often against her.

In such a world, the people did not need vague spirituality or disconnected communities. They needed a Church that was visible, grounded, and unified. A Church that could teach with authority, correct with compassion, and protect the flock entrusted to her care. They needed the *Catholic* Church—not as a name for a new religion, but as the embodiment of the fullness of the faith passed down from the apostles.

This is why the Church was never merely a loose association of believers. It had order. It had structure. It had bishops and priests—spiritual fathers who could guide, correct, baptize, and nourish the people in the sacraments. The Body of Christ was not meant to scatter when challenged. It was meant to stand—one, holy, catholic, and apostolic.

The councils, creeds, and defenses of the faith that would follow did not arise in academic boredom or philosophical pride. They came as a response to real dangers. In every generation, new distortions would emerge—teachings that *sounded* faithful but led people away from the truth. These heresies rarely began as open rebellions. More often, they began as sincere but misguided interpretations of who Christ was, what salvation meant, or how grace worked.

The Church's responses were never about grasping for power or inventing new dogmas. Rather, they were rooted in the deep awareness that souls were at stake. When teachings arose that twisted or diluted the truth of Christ, the Church could not remain silent. Her role was to guard the deposit of faith—not as a museum curator, but as a living, breathing witness to what had been received from the apostles. With courage and conviction, she stepped into the confusion—not to stifle thought, but to illuminate the path back to what had always been true.

Confronting the Storm: Defending the Truth in Tumultuous Times

In the centuries following the apostolic era, the Christian faith spread across cultures and borders, but so too did misunderstandings, distortions, and deliberate rejections of essential truths. Heresies did not always arise from malice. In many cases, they were born of sincere —but misguided—attempts to explain divine mysteries. These deviations stirred confusion, challenged the faithful, and threatened the unity of the Church. And so, a pattern began to emerge: when controversy arose, the bishops of the Church, united with the Bishop of Rome, would come together to clarify, correct, and reaffirm the truth that had been handed down from the apostles.

One of the earliest examples was the heresy of Arianism, which denied the full divinity of Jesus Christ. Arius, a priest in Alexandria in the early fourth century, taught that the Son of God was a created being—higher than man, but not equal to the Father. This doctrine spread rapidly, gaining support even from emperors and high-ranking officials. The stakes were enormous: if Jesus were not truly God, then He could not redeem humanity. If He were merely a creature, then the entire Gospel message would collapse.

It was at the First Council of Nicaea in 325 A.D. that the Church decisively responded. Convened by Emperor Constantine but governed by the bishops, the council condemned Arianism and proclaimed that the Son is "consubstantial with the Father"—fully God, equal in divinity, uncreated and eternal. This affirmation would find its way into the Nicene Creed, which Catholics and many other Christians still recite today.

Other challenges followed. The Nestorian controversy in the fifth century attempted to divide Christ's human and divine natures so severely that it threatened the unity of His person. The Church responded at the Council of Ephesus in 431 A.D., affirming that Jesus is one divine person with two natures, and upholding the title of Mary as *Theotokos*—God-bearer—because the child she bore was truly God in the flesh.

Shortly thereafter, the Monophysite heresy claimed the opposite—that Christ's divinity absorbed His humanity entirely, leaving Him with only one nature. At the Council of Chalcedon in 451 A.D., the Church reaffirmed the fullness of both natures—divine and human—united in one Person, without confusion, change, division, or separation.

These controversies were not abstract theological arguments. They were battles for the soul of Christianity—battles that had real consequences for real people. They were also moments that demonstrated why the Church's hierarchical structure, the authority of bishops, and the primacy of the Bishop of Rome were not merely symbolic, but essential.

Unity Under Fire: The Church Holds the Line

As the Church faced external threats and internal pressures, the call for unity became more than an ideal—it was a lifeline. Doctrinal disputes such as Arianism, Nestorianism, and Monophysitism threatened to fracture the Church's theological foundations. While the Eastern centers of learning often provided the deep theological vocabulary to articulate orthodox responses, it was the unity between these efforts and the pastoral confirmation of Rome that gave the Church her strength and cohesion.

Rome did not serve as a passive rubber stamp, nor was the East the sole source of theological clarity. The Catholic Church, by design, was not regional but universal—capable of drawing together bishops and thinkers from every corner of the Christian world. When the bishop of Rome confirmed the decrees of the councils, it wasn't a political move—it was a pastoral one. It reminded the Church, east and west, that unity was both possible and necessary.

This didn't mean every pope was always a model of holiness. Some fell short in virtue or became entangled in the political currents of their day. The same can be said of many bishops, East and West alike. But when the Church needed to act decisively to safeguard the deposit of faith, the Holy Spirit ensured that the truth remained unadulterated. No amount of personal frailty or political maneuvering could override the divine protection Christ gave to His Church.

In that sense, conciliar decisions mattered most when they were in union with the bishop of Rome. His approval wasn't a formality—it was the sign that the Church had spoken in harmony. And for the faithful—many of whom could neither read nor access the theological intricacies debated in the councils—this unity was a source of clarity and peace. If the pope and the bishops together had affirmed it, the people could trust it.

Even as the Church operated across empires, languages, and cultures, her unity remained intact. But tensions were beginning to rise—tensions that would eventually strain the very relationship that had safeguarded the truth. And while many look back and see a split that was inevitable, the reality is far more tragic and complex. The Church was still one. Still guided by the same Spirit. Still breathing, but with growing difficulty.

Chapter 10

The Shepherd's Burden: Preserving Unity in Crisis

A Guardian in the Storm

The early Church had endured much—persecution, martyrdom, dispersion. And yet, under the guidance of the apostles and their successors, she grew in faith, number, and mission.

But what happens when the danger no longer comes from outside—but rises from confusion within?

False teachings—heresies—began to swirl. Some were born of misunderstanding; others were encouraged by political agendas. Some were met with firm resistance. Others—unfortunately—were met with compromise.

The Eastern Church, celebrated for its rich theological and monastic tradition, found itself in a delicate dance with imperial authority. Emperors like Constantius II and later Valens supported theological views that opposed the Nicene faith. Bishops were pressured, exiled, or replaced depending on whether their theology aligned with the reigning ruler.

And at this critical juncture, the Church turned again toward Rome.

Arianism and the Need for Rome

Arianism denied the eternal divinity of Christ, claiming He was a created being—exalted, yes, but not consubstantial with the Father. The heresy spread rapidly, especially under the protection of sympathetic emperors.

Even bishops who had once stood firmly with Nicaea found themselves worn down.

St. Hilary of Poitiers wrote of the eastern churches at the time:

"The ears of the people have grown accustomed to heresy."

—*Ad Constantium*, II.8

Some Eastern bishops, including Eusebius of Nicomedia, George of Cappadocia, and Ursacius and Valens of Illyria, embraced Arian sympathies, while others—like St. Athanasius of Alexandria—were exiled multiple times for defending the Nicene faith. The Synod of Antioch (341), under imperial pressure, produced creeds that subtly avoided the term *homoousios* ("of the same substance") to appease the Arians.

In this climate, Rome remained a steady voice.

Pope Julius I (r. 337–352), receiving letters from both Arian and Nicene parties, replied clearly:

"It behoves us not to make a departure from the faith... but to preserve what has been handed down to us from the beginning."

—Letter of Pope Julius I to the Eastern Bishops (c. 341)

He later convened the Synod of Rome (342) which exonerated Athanasius, condemned the Arian-leaning factions, and refused to accept creeds not consistent with the Nicene formula.

Rome, still distant from the imperial seat of power, had not compromised.

The Iconoclast Crisis—Rome's Steady Voice

In the eighth century, a new storm emerged—not over councils or creeds, but over images. Sacred images.

The veneration of icons—especially in the East—had become central to the devotional life of the faithful. These weren't merely decorative works of art; they were windows into heaven. Icons told the stories of Scripture, the saints, and salvation. In a time when many people could not read, and Bibles were only painstakingly hand-printed and not able to be owned by every individual Christian, icons proclaimed the Gospel through color, symbol, and silence.

They taught. They comforted. They helped the poor and unlettered to *see* the Word of God.

And more than that, they affirmed the deepest truth of the Incarnation—that God had truly taken on visible, physical flesh in Jesus Christ. If God had made His face visible in Christ, then it was no sin to depict His human face in sacred art. The veneration of icons was never idolatry. Christians did not worship wood or paint—they honored the person whom the image represented.

As St. Basil the Great wrote:

"The honor paid to the image passes to the prototype; and whoever venerates the image, venerates in it the reality of what is represented."

—St. Basil, *On the Holy Spirit*, 18.45

But not everyone understood.

The Byzantine Emperor Leo III, and later his son Constantine V, issued imperial edicts forbidding the use of icons. Churches were stripped bare. Monasteries were persecuted. Defenders of icons were branded heretics or enemies of the empire.

Under pressure from the state, many Eastern bishops fell silent—or worse, joined the movement of iconoclasm (literally, "image-breaking").

And again, the eyes of the faithful turned to Rome.

Pope Gregory II (r. 715–731) resisted the emperor's demands, defending the long-standing practice of honoring images of Christ and the saints. His successor, Pope Gregory III, went even further. In 731, he convened a synod in Rome that condemned iconoclasm as heresy and excommunicated those who denied the rightful veneration of sacred images.

Rome's response was not innovation—it was fidelity.

Papal legates would later attend the Seventh Ecumenical Council, the Second Council of Nicaea in 787, which decisively resolved the controversy. There, the Church affirmed:

> "We define... that just as the figure of the precious and life-giving cross, so also the venerable and holy images... are to be exhibited in the holy churches of God... For the honor which is given to the image passes on to that which the image represents."

—Second Council of Nicaea, *Definition of Faith*, 787

Through this, the Church declared again that Christ's Incarnation was not symbolic—it was real. Heaven had shown its face. And we were never meant to forget it.

A Growing Tension

Yet here lies the paradox: these moments of necessary intervention by Rome sometimes caused discomfort in the East—especially when decisions came with finality.

The same Rome that had offered clarity in times of confusion was now being scrutinized more closely by Eastern leaders who, though still respectful, grew increasingly wary of what they perceived as Roman centralization.

Still, history shows that Rome's presence, its witness, and its decisions were essential to preserving unity in crisis.

As the next centuries unfolded, it would become harder to hold that unity together. But Rome's role had already been made clear.

Not perfect in every pastoral act—but faithful in the protection of divine truth.

Constantinople's Rise and Rivalry

As the centuries passed, the city of Constantinople grew not only in imperial stature but in ecclesial ambition. Founded by Emperor Constantine in the fourth century as "Nova Roma" (New Rome), Constantinople became the seat of political power in the East. It was a city envisioned as both a Christian capital and a beacon of imperial glory. The emperor lived there, the senate moved there, and eventually, the Eastern Church would come to revolve around it.

But with its political prestige came ecclesial aspirations. While the Bishop of Rome had long been honored for his apostolic foundation—tracing his lineage to Peter himself—the bishop of Constantinople began to be seen as second in rank, not due to apostolic heritage, but because of the city's political prominence. This was made official at the Council of Constantinople in 381, where it was declared that the bishop of Constantinople should have the "second place in honor" after Rome, *because* it was the new capital.

Rome accepted the bishop's elevated role in dignity but not in jurisdiction. Apostolic origin, not imperial geography, had always been the measure of authority in the Church. The sees of Antioch, Alexandria, and Jerusalem had ancient roots, but only Rome could claim the Petrine foundation in unbroken succession.

Still, Constantinople's influence grew. Over time, its patriarch came to exercise increasing authority over other eastern regions—claiming jurisdiction that traditionally belonged to older apostolic sees. This centralization caused friction not only with Rome but also with bishops in Alexandria, Antioch, and Jerusalem. What emerged was not a united Eastern front, but rather a competition among centers of power.

In many ways, Constantinople became a symbol of both the brilliance and the burden of the Eastern Church. It was the home of profound theological thought, stunning liturgical expression, and vibrant Christian life. But it was also a place where ecclesial politics and imperial influence became deeply intertwined. The Byzantine emperors often saw themselves as defenders of orthodoxy, yet they sometimes imposed theological policies through force, as seen in the Iconoclast controversy and earlier Christological disputes. Bishops who resisted imperial heresies could face exile, imprisonment, or worse.

Rome, distant from the reach of the Eastern emperors, provided a necessary refuge of stability. The Bishop of Rome, though not immune to political pressures of the West, could often stand firm when Eastern bishops were muzzled or manipulated. This dynamic —Rome as a refuge for doctrinal clarity—would re-emerge time and again throughout Church history.

While Constantinople's rise was not inherently problematic, its influence introduced a new challenge to the unity of the Church. In time, rivalry turned to resistance. Disagreements became doctrinal standoffs. And what had once been a complementary partnership between East and West began to fracture under the weight of pride, politics, and persistent misunderstanding.

The Filioque Flashpoint

One of the most enduring flashpoints between East and West came from a single Latin word: *Filioque*—meaning "and the Son."

Originally, the Nicene Creed (formalized in A.D. 325 and expanded at Constantinople in 381) declared that the Holy Spirit "proceeds from the Father." This language reflected the words of Jesus in John 15:26: *"When the Counselor comes, whom I shall send to you from the Father, even the Spirit of truth, who proceeds from the Father…"*

However, as heresies in the West—especially Arianism—challenged the full divinity of the Son, Western bishops began using the phrase *"who proceeds from the Father and the Son"* to defend the eternal unity and equality of the Father and the Son. It was a theological clarification, not a contradiction. The Spirit proceeds from the Father as the source, but not independently of the Son. The Father sends the Spirit *through* the Son. This is consistent with other scriptural testimony, such as Romans 8:9 and Galatians 4:6, where the Holy Spirit is referred to as the Spirit of Christ and the one sent into our hearts by the Son.

By the sixth century, the *Filioque* phrase had begun appearing in creeds used in some parts of the Latin-speaking Church, especially in Spain and Gaul. In the early ninth century, it received renewed attention under the influence of Charlemagne, the Frankish king crowned Emperor of the Romans by Pope Leo III in A.D. 800. Charlemagne sought to unify the Western Church under a strong and clearly defined orthodoxy, and he championed the *Filioque* as a necessary expression of the Son's full divinity—an effort to combat lingering Arian influences in his realm. Though Pope Leo III was cautious about adding the phrase to the official creed recited in Rome, he nonetheless had two silver plaques engraved with the original form of the creed (without *Filioque*) and mounted them at St. Peter's Basilica —an effort to preserve the council's original wording while also affirming the orthodoxy of the Western understanding. Eventually, the phrase gained broader acceptance in the Latin liturgy, especially as the need for clarity in the face of heresy continued to grow. To many in the East, however, the addition of *Filioque* represented an unauthorized alteration of a creed established by ecumenical councils. Their concern was twofold: first, that the creed was being changed without an ecumenical gathering; second, that the theology itself might imply two sources of the Spirit, thus diminishing the unique role of the Father.

Rome, for its part, clarified that *Filioque* did not mean the Holy Spirit proceeds from *two origins*, but rather from the Father *through* the Son—an ancient formulation used even by Eastern Fathers like St. Cyril of Alexandria. The Pope's intention was not to dominate, but to defend the fullness of Trinitarian doctrine in response to Western heresies that were undermining the Son's divinity.

But theological precision could not overcome growing political and cultural mistrust. The East saw the West as arrogant; the West saw the East as rigid. The doctrinal debate was real, but it became a battleground for deeper wounds—language barriers, ecclesial rivalry, and geopolitical competition.

The *Filioque* controversy did not rupture communion overnight. It smoldered for centuries. Yet it became emblematic of a broader question: Who has the authority to define and preserve doctrine? For the West, the See of Peter had that role. For the East, no single bishop could unilaterally impose a change—especially one that touched the creed itself.

In time, the issue would surface again and again—sometimes with theological sincerity, sometimes with political provocation. And when the formal split came in 1054, *Filioque* would stand as one of the key differences cited.

But as we'll see, the schism wasn't caused by theology alone. The creed may have cracked on paper, but the deeper fracture was between brothers—between bishops who no longer trusted one another to carry the burden of unity together.

Despite Rome's perseverance in maintaining unity amid theological storms, the landscape of Christendom was changing. The growing distance—both geographical and philosophical—between East and West created more than just misunderstanding. It laid down roots of mistrust that were slow to heal. The Bishop of Rome, once a sign of shared confirmation across all Christendom, was now increasingly viewed through the lens of rivalry by some in the East, especially as his voice continued to carry weight even in their internal disputes.

Yet for all the controversies and power struggles, what remained unchanged was the mission of the Church. The Gospel still burned in the hearts of believers. The sacraments still poured out grace. The Church still stood—wounded, yet not destroyed.

And so we reach a critical turning point.

The stage was set for a theological rupture that would push East and West further apart. At the heart of it: one phrase—*Filioque*—just three words in Latin, but words that would ignite a firestorm of theological and political consequence. The story of that division, and how it shaped the path of the Church for centuries to come, now demands our full attention.

Chapter 11

The Great Schism: A House Divided

I t didn't happen in a single moment.

The break between East and West unfolded like a long and sorrowful goodbye—one that neither side could bring itself to make cleanly. For centuries, tensions had been growing, cooled by occasional reconciliation but reignited by misunderstanding, cultural division, political ambition, and theological dispute.

The final fracture came in 1054—but it wasn't the beginning. It was the culmination.

By then, Constantinople had grown into a powerful and self-assured patriarchate, viewing itself not only as the center of the Eastern Church, but as the beating heart of Christian civilization. Rome, meanwhile, had weathered waves of persecution, doctrinal challenges, political interference, and heresy. Yet through it all, the bishop of Rome continued to be seen—even by many in the East—as the figure who bore Peter's commission.

But as the centuries passed, unity frayed.

Theological debates—like the inclusion of the *filioque* clause in the Nicene Creed ("and the Son")—played a role. So did differences in language, custom, and liturgy. But at the heart of the divide was the question of primacy.

Was the pope simply the *first among equals*? Or did he possess a unique authority granted by Christ himself? That question haunted both the theological halls of East and West and the corridors of empire. And when Pope Leo IX sent envoys to Constantinople to settle rising tensions, what followed was not peace—but excommunication.

The formal breach of 1054 marked a painful turning point. While both sides continued to affirm the Creed, the Scriptures, and apostolic succession, they now did so in isolation from one another.

A single Body, divided.

A wound in the Church that, nearly a thousand years later, still aches.

Yet even here, we see evidence not of two faiths, but two lungs of the same Body that had forgotten how to breathe together. The truths of the faith remained intact. The sacraments were not undone. But unity was lost.

And in the pain of that loss, a new question would emerge:

Could the wound be healed?

The Church had weathered storms before—heresies, persecutions, political interference—but none threatened the visible unity of Christendom as profoundly as the rift now forming between East and West.

This was not a sudden break, but a slow unraveling—a deep and painful wound that emerged after centuries of shared faith, mutual councils, and apostolic succession. And at the heart of this unraveling was not simply theological disagreement, but something more human: miscommunication, wounded pride, geopolitical posturing, and a growing unease with the office of Peter.

For many centuries, the East had looked to Rome not as a rival, but as a reference point—a bishopric that, through the See of Peter, offered stability and confirmation. The Bishop of Rome had often validated the great councils, supported the Eastern Fathers in moments of heretical threat, and embraced the universal mission of the Church.

But times had changed.

As Constantinople grew in prominence, as the Byzantine emperors asserted more control over ecclesiastical decisions, and as cultural differences deepened, something began to shift. Rome was still revered—but also resented. Eastern bishops, confident in their theology and traditions, became increasingly wary of what they perceived as overreach. And when papal decisions contradicted Eastern customs or appeared unilateral, suspicion gave way to accusation.

Even the phrase *first among equals*, once a generous affirmation of Petrine primacy, became a shield—used to protect local authority more than to celebrate unity. The East had not yet fully rejected Rome's role, but it had grown uncomfortable with how that role was expressed.

This discomfort would soon boil over.

A series of flashpoints—some theological, others political, many deeply personal—would bring the tension to a head. And what had once been a family struggling to understand itself would, in time, become a house divided.

The road to the Great Schism was not paved by one decision, one bishop, or one dispute. It was the result of a long series of missed opportunities, stubborn egos, and differing visions of what it meant to be one, holy, catholic, and apostolic.

But before the break came, there was still a chance for healing.

Key Players Emerge

By the middle of the 11th century, centuries of tension had accumulated between the Eastern and Western Churches. While the theological foundations remained largely the same, the relationship had grown strained. The Church in the West, rooted in Latin language, Roman law, and papal primacy, continued to assert itself as the guardian of universal unity. The East, deeply embedded in Byzantine tradition, Greek culture, and imperial influence, maintained a strong regional identity—one that no longer found comfort in Roman oversight.

It was during this fragile moment that two towering figures would clash.

Pope Leo IX, elected in 1049, was a reform-minded pontiff. He sought to purify the Church of simony, enforce clerical celibacy, and strengthen papal authority—not only in the West, but across the entire Christian world. To him, the unity of the Church was not a matter of diplomacy but of divine order. Peter had been given the keys, and those keys were not ornamental—they were binding.

On the other side of the divide was Patriarch Michael Cerularius of Constantinople, a fiercely independent and politically astute leader. He was no stranger to controversy and had little patience for what he viewed as Western arrogance. To Cerularius, the rising claims of the Roman pope were not signs of leadership, but of intrusion. While he did not deny Rome's historical significance, he bristled at the idea that the East should submit to Western reforms or customs, especially those not shared by the broader Eastern Church.

And while theological disagreements certainly existed, it was not doctrine alone that sparked the final fire.

It was personalities, politics, and posturing.

Pope Leo, determined to assert Rome's authority, sent a delegation to Constantinople in 1054. Leading that delegation was Cardinal Humbert of Silva Candida, a man known for his intellect—and his temper. He was not the ideal choice for bridge-building. Though deeply loyal to Rome, Humbert lacked the subtlety required for delicate diplomacy. His approach was confrontational, not conciliatory.

What followed was not a council or a conversation—it was a collision.

The meeting between Cardinal Humbert and Patriarch Cerularius quickly devolved into mutual accusations and ecclesiastical chest-thumping. Neither side was willing to concede. Humbert eventually marched into the Hagia Sophia—Constantinople's great cathedral—and placed a bull of excommunication on the altar, condemning Cerularius and his allies. In response, Cerularius held a synod that excommunicated Humbert and his delegation.

Neither side fully understood the implications of that day.

At first, it seemed like just another skirmish in a long and uneasy relationship. But this time, the breach did not heal. The wounds festered. And the line that had once been blurred was now drawn.

The Great Schism had begun.

A House Divided

By the time 1054 arrived, the unity that once marked the Christian world had frayed beyond repair. What had begun as occasional disagreements between Rome and Constantinople had grown into an ever-widening distance. This wasn't simply a clash of doctrines—it was a breakdown in relationship. For generations, the Church had wrestled with contrasting customs, divergent languages, and competing sources of influence. The West leaned toward Latin precision and legal expression; the East embraced Greek nuance and mystical contemplation. Over time, these differences shaped two distinct ways of thinking about authority, liturgy, and even the very nature of unity itself.

Still, the fracture did not have to be final.

The moment of excommunication between Cardinal Humbert and Patriarch Michael Cerularius was dramatic, but in many ways, symbolic. Neither man held the power to truly break the Church in two. And yet their actions formalized what had already become a painful reality: the churches of the East and West no longer moved together in step. Rome continued to affirm the primacy of Peter's successor as a divinely instituted office essential to the unity of the Church. The East began to view that same office with suspicion, especially as geopolitical pressures and theological pride deepened the rift.

The tragedy of the Schism is not merely historical—it is deeply spiritual. Two lungs of the same body ceased breathing in harmony. Two brothers at the same table now dined apart. And the global Church has felt the weight of that separation ever since.

The Aftermath and Attempts at Reconciliation

Despite the formal split, efforts at reunion surfaced repeatedly. The Church did not accept the rupture as permanent. Councils like Lyons in 1274 and Florence in 1439 succeeded—on paper—in reconciling the East and West. Eastern bishops signed declarations affirming communion with the pope and the doctrines of the Catholic faith. But the joy was short-lived.

The people of the East, especially the monastics and clergy outside the council chambers, rejected these agreements. Many felt the West had imposed terms rather than sought mutual understanding. In some cases, emperors and bishops accepted reunion not out of conviction, but desperation—hoping to secure military aid from the West against Turkish threats.

Rome, for its part, genuinely sought to repair the breach, but often misread the emotional and cultural wounds involved. The result was a fragile peace that could not hold.

Centuries passed. Theologies became more rigid. Suspicions hardened. And the once-shared story of a universal Church became a divided memory.

In a moment of modern grace, Pope Paul VI and Patriarch Athenagoras I, in 1965, lifted the mutual excommunications from 1054. It was a gesture that acknowledged how deeply the division had wounded the Church—but also how much hope still remained.

Bridging Toward Hope

Though the formal rupture between East and West became more pronounced after 1054, the story of the Church did not end in separation. Instead, it carried forward—often painfully, sometimes in silence, and occasionally in deep dialogue. Remarkably, even after the split, the influence and importance of the pope did not disappear from the East entirely.

One significant moment came nearly four centuries later, at the Council of Florence (1439). In a time of desperation, as the Eastern Roman Empire faced collapse before advancing Ottoman forces, bishops from both East and West gathered to discuss the possibility of healing the breach. There, under the leadership of Pope Eugene IV, theological agreement was reached on long-divisive issues: the Filioque, purgatory, and papal primacy. Though the union ultimately collapsed under pressure from Eastern political and monastic opposition, the very fact that bishops and theologians from both sides entered into real, respectful theological dialogue is a testament to the enduring importance of unity under the guidance of the successor of Peter.

Even more enduring has been the witness of those Eastern Churches who chose communion with Rome. These Eastern Catholic Churches—sometimes called "Uniate" Churches, though the term can carry pejorative connotations—represent ancient Christian communities that retained their liturgical rites, languages, and canonical disciplines while affirming full communion with the Holy See. They are not Roman Catholics who use a different ritual; they are fully Catholic and fully Eastern.

Some of the most prominent Eastern Catholic Churches include:

• The Maronite Catholic Church – With roots in Lebanon and Syria, the Maronites never formally broke communion with Rome, and to this day they preserve their rich Syriac liturgy and identity while professing union with the pope.

• The Ukrainian Greek Catholic Church – The largest Eastern Catholic Church today, it follows the Byzantine rite and was formed in 1596 through the Union of Brest. Despite intense persecution, especially under communism, Ukrainian Catholics have remained steadfast in faith and in communion with Rome.

• The Melkite Greek Catholic Church – Originating in the Near East, the Melkites also follow the Byzantine liturgy and emphasize their identity as both Eastern and Catholic. Their name reflects loyalty to the "king" (emperor) and, eventually, to Rome.

• The Chaldean Catholic Church – Rooted in ancient Mesopotamia, this Church follows the East Syriac Rite and is prominent in Iraq and among diaspora communities around the world.

There are more: the Syro-Malabar and Syro-Malankara Catholics of India, the Armenian Catholic Church, the Coptic Catholic Church of Egypt, and others. These communities are a living bridge between East and West, offering proof that unity is possible without uniformity.

The popes of more recent centuries have not ignored these Churches. In fact, Pope Leo XIII, in his 1894 apostolic letter *Orientalium Dignitas*, forcefully defended the dignity and autonomy of the Eastern Catholic Churches, writing:

"The Churches of the East are the most venerable among us... It is Our wish that the ancient rite of each Church be held in due honor."

This spirit of respect and dialogue continued in the 20th century, especially under Pope St. John Paul II, who famously reminded the world that the Church must "breathe with both lungs—the East and the West." He vigorously supported Eastern Catholics and extended heartfelt invitations to the Orthodox to rediscover unity not by abandoning their tradition, but by embracing the full communion that Christ desired for His Church.

So while wounds remain, they are not without signs of healing. The very existence of Eastern Catholic Churches, together with the respectful dialogue of recent popes and Orthodox patriarchs, gives us reason to hope. The papacy, even in times of estrangement, has continued to shine as a visible sign of unity—a reminder of Christ's words to Peter, "Strengthen your brethren" (Luke 22:32).

And so the story presses forward. Though the Great Schism remains one of the most painful episodes in Christian history, bridges have never stopped being built. Some have been walked across. Others remain under construction. But the Catholic Church, East and West, continues to long for the day when Jesus' prayer will be fulfilled:

"That they may all be one; even as You, Father, are in Me and I in You" (John 17:21).

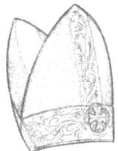  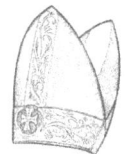

Chapter 12

Liturgies of Light through Shadows of Division

A Holy, Apostolic Church—But Not Yet Whole

The Orthodox Church today remains a revered and sacred body, upholding apostolic succession, valid sacraments, and a profound liturgical tradition. But structurally, it functions as a communion of self-governing Churches without a central authority capable of resolving disputes definitively. What was once a strength—its rootedness in national and regional identity—has, over time, made it vulnerable to fractures, rivalries, and political entanglements.

The Russian Orthodox Church (ROC) is a prime example. Its decision in 2018 to sever communion with the Ecumenical Patriarch of Constantinople over the granting of autocephaly (self-governance) to the Orthodox Church of Ukraine (OCU) demonstrated the limits of unity without a binding voice. The ROC's alignment with the Russian state, particularly during the war in Ukraine, has left many questioning whether faith or nationalism holds greater sway.

While Orthodoxy safeguards much of the early Church's external form—iconography, chant, fasting rhythms, and liturgical depth—it suffers internally from the absence of a unified shepherding structure.

By contrast, the Catholic Church, centered in Rome, has endured its own share of trials—scandals, reformations, and even unworthy leaders. But her doctrinal unity and spiritual depth have never been lost. The papacy remains a visible and enduring safeguard of truth, established by Christ not to dominate, but to confirm, anchor, and unify. Even when some leaders failed in holiness, the teaching office entrusted to Peter and his successors has never led the faithful astray on matters of faith and morals.

The Catholic Church, like the Church of the East, has saints, mystics, and martyrs. She has given the world the Divine Mercy devotion, Eucharistic miracles, and Marian apparitions that continue to call hearts to repentance and intimacy with God. Her beauty is not confined to the basilica but is found in the Catechism, the Rosary, the Sacraments, and the unbroken witness of truth.

Pope Benedict XVI, deeply respectful of the Eastern tradition, once reflected:

"Without a primacy anchored in the Eucharist and the episcopate, and centered in a bishop who is the visible sign of unity, the Church can become a federation of local churches with no real unity"

(*Principles of Catholic Theology*, 1982).

This is not said with pride, but with humble longing—not for domination, but for reunion. A Church divided is a Church wounded. But a Church united in truth is a force the world cannot overcome.

Chapter 13

The Reformers and the Rock

Reformation or Rejection?

By the early 1500s, Europe was shifting — intellectually, politically, and spiritually. The Renaissance had sparked a renewed interest in learning, the arts, and personal responsibility. Nationalism was growing. Monarchs were asserting independence. And a rising tide of religious fervor — mixed with frustration — was beginning to challenge authority.

It was in this atmosphere of change, not collapse, that the Catholic Church found herself facing both scrutiny and slander.

It's important to clarify from the start: the doctrine of indulgences is not — and never was — the problem. Indulgences are rooted in sound theology: the Church's authority to bind and loose (cf. Matthew 16:19), the reality of temporal consequences for sin, and the communion of saints by which the merits of Christ and the faithful are shared for the good of souls. Properly understood, indulgences are spiritual aids — not shortcuts to salvation.

But as with any spiritual discipline, misunderstanding and misapplication can lead to abuse. And so they did — not by official Church teaching, but by local clerics and preachers who promoted indulgences with little or no catechesis. Some blurred the lines between making a voluntary offering and receiving spiritual benefit, allowing a false narrative to take hold: that indulgences could be "bought."

In reality, the Church never sold indulgences. But in certain regions, especially within the German territories, the appearance of spiritual commerce led to confusion. A wealthy man might assume that his donation to fund a chapel or project had secured his freedom from purgatory — not because the Church taught this, but because someone poorly explained it... or failed to explain it at all.

These local abuses were scandalous and harmful, but they were not representative of universal Catholic practice, nor were they unchallenged. Reformers within the Church herself — theologians, bishops, and even popes — had already begun addressing the need for clearer catechesis and pastoral reform.

But the fire had started, and one man in Wittenberg would soon strike a match that couldn't be contained.

The Troubled Soul of Martin Luther

Martin Luther was not a villain. He was not a power-hungry rebel, nor a man seeking to destroy the Church he had grown up loving. In many ways, he was quite the opposite — a deeply spiritual man tormented by a profound and unrelenting fear of damnation.

Born in 1483 in Eisleben, Germany, Luther was the son of a strict and ambitious father who wanted him to become a lawyer. But a violent thunderstorm in 1505 changed the course of his life. Fearing for his soul as lightning crashed around him, the young Luther cried out to St. Anne, promising to become a monk if his life were spared.

He kept that promise, entering the Augustinian order shortly thereafter.

Luther was devout — almost obsessively so. He prayed constantly, fasted rigorously, and confessed his sins with such scrupulous detail that even his confessors reportedly grew weary. He once said, *"If anyone could have earned heaven by the life of a monk, it was I."* Yet the more he pursued holiness, the more aware he became of his failings. His conscience was not quieted by his religious devotion — it was inflamed by it.

At the heart of Luther's torment was a single question: *How can a sinner ever be justified before a righteous God?*

This question haunted him. Despite his priesthood, his theological training, and his monastic life, Luther could not find peace. The system of penance, indulgences, and acts of contrition — all rooted in centuries of Catholic tradition — offered no assurance to his deeply burdened conscience.

As a professor of theology at the University of Wittenberg, Luther began to study Scripture with intensity. It was here that he developed a profound attachment to St. Paul's writings, especially the epistle to the Romans. The verse that struck him most was Romans 1:17: *"He who through faith is righteous shall live."* This became the bedrock of his theology: justification by faith alone (*sola fide*).

But Luther's personal conversion — and theological breakthrough — would soon bring him into direct conflict with the Catholic Church, particularly when it came to the nature of authority, the means of grace, and the ministry of the pope.

Still, in the early stages, Luther didn't see himself as leaving the Church. Rather, he hoped to call it back to what he saw as the heart of the Gospel. His now-famous *Ninety-Five Theses*, posted on October 31, 1517, were intended as a scholarly invitation to debate. He wanted dialogue, not division. His main concern at the time was the misuse and misunderstanding of indulgences — a valid concern shared by many others within the Church. Luther believed these abuses obscured the Gospel and exploited the faithful.

What followed, however, was far more than debate. The fire Luther lit would grow into a blaze that would engulf much of Europe and forever alter the course of Christianity.

From Reform to Rebellion: How Conviction Turned to Conflict

It's important to remember that Martin Luther did not set out to start a new church. In his early years as a monk and theologian, he believed himself to be a faithful son of the Church, grappling with age-old questions about grace, justification, and human weakness. His emphasis on faith, humility, and personal prayer was not immediately at odds with Catholic doctrine. In fact, his reverence for Scripture and passion for moral reform echoed the cries of many Catholic saints and thinkers before him.

What changed? In part, it was the cultural and ecclesial climate in which he found himself.

Luther witnessed firsthand the abuse of indulgences—not their theological foundation, which the Church affirmed and still does, but the way they were being marketed to the faithful as if they were spiritual commodities. Preachers like Johann Tetzel, famously associated with the phrase *"As soon as the coin in the coffer rings, a soul from purgatory springs,"* were exploiting people's fears for financial gain. This was not the official position of the Church, but the sloppy or corrupt application of it in certain regions, often driven by local clerics under financial pressure.

Luther was not alone in his concern. Many faithful Catholics agreed that reform was necessary. But when Luther sought to address these abuses through debate and dialogue, including appeals to the pope, he felt dismissed—misunderstood at best, censured at worst. The frustration he experienced in trying to provoke internal correction began to harden his tone. The scholar's pen slowly gave way to the polemicist's sword.

Over time, Luther's emphasis on faith and Scripture became more than a corrective within the Church—they became battle lines drawn against her authority. Where once he may have hoped to renew the Church from within, he now accused her of having lost her way altogether. This shift was not theological in origin, but relational and political.

It was not doctrine alone that divided the Body of Christ, but hurt, pride, misunderstanding, and unresolved tension. What could have remained an internal renewal became an external rupture.

Indulgences: What the Church Really Taught — and Still Teaches

Indulgences were never meant to be "spiritual shortcuts" or items to be bought and sold. Contrary to common belief, the Catholic Church has never taught that forgiveness, salvation, or time off in purgatory can be purchased with money.

What, then, is an indulgence?

An indulgence is the remission before God of the temporal punishment due to sins whose guilt has already been forgiven (cf. *Catechism of the Catholic Church*, 1471). In other words, it does not forgive sin — only the sacrament of Confession does that — but it acknowledges that even forgiven sin carries consequences. Those consequences may be purified through prayer, penance, acts of charity, or, yes, indulgences granted by the Church through certain pious acts done with the proper disposition.

To draw an analogy: If a child breaks a window, the parent may forgive him — but the window still needs to be repaired. The repair doesn't earn the forgiveness, but it restores what was damaged. So it is with indulgences. They are acts that heal what was wounded, not purchases of God's mercy.

The Church, as the steward of the treasures of grace entrusted to her by Christ, has always taught that indulgences must be rooted in genuine contrition, prayer, sacramental confession, and acts of charity or devotion. During certain points in history, the Church even offered indulgences to those who supported good causes — such as building hospitals or churches — but always under the assumption that the donation was freely given in faith and good will, not as a bribe or transaction.

Unfortunately, this theology was not always communicated clearly to the faithful, especially during the late medieval period. In certain places — particularly in the German territories where Luther lived — some preachers reduced indulgences to a kind of spiritual marketplace, presenting them as guarantees of pardon in exchange for financial support. While Church councils and popes had condemned such abuse repeatedly, the catechetical breakdown and clerical misapplication created a spiritual crisis.

Luther was right to call attention to the abuse. But in rejecting the abuse, he rejected the theology as well. And in doing so, he ultimately rejected the authority of the Church to teach, interpret, and administer the mercy of Christ.

From Protest to Rejection: The 95 Theses and the Breaking of Authority

When Martin Luther composed his 95 Theses, he did so not as a man seeking to shatter the unity of the Church, but as a professor of theology and Augustinian monk who believed in the Church's power to correct itself. His concerns centered around the abuse of indulgences, not the legitimacy of the Church itself. At first.

But everything changed when his challenge to certain clerical abuses—particularly the aggressive promotion of indulgences in Germany—was met not with dialogue, but with condemnation.

Luther's theses, written in Latin and intended for academic discussion, were quickly translated and spread across Europe thanks to the printing press. Rather than being received as theological critique within the family of the Church, his writings began to stir popular unrest and feed growing resentment toward Church hierarchy. In response, Rome defended the authority of the pope, asserting that indulgences, rightly understood and applied, were part of the Church's treasury of grace—not a commodity to be abused or bartered.

It was Luther's refusal to submit to the pope's correction that marked the true rupture.

This became a familiar pattern: when challenged by the teaching authority of the Church, some individuals or movements chose to reject the authority itself rather than accept correction. Disagreement, once seen as something to resolve within the Body of Christ, now became justification for walking away.

If there is no infallible authority, then every person becomes their own arbiter of truth. And if that's the case, then no disagreement ever truly needs to be reconciled—just renamed, rebranded, and released as the next independent Christian community.

And so it happened. The protest became Protestantism, and Protestantism became proliferation.

Without the anchor of apostolic authority, division became inevitable. What began as one man's protest quickly multiplied into tens of thousands of denominations, each claiming to be rooted in the same Gospel, yet differing in doctrine, sacrament, and moral teaching.

And still today, the issue of authority remains at the heart of the divide. The Church's claim that Christ gave Peter a unique, ongoing role of leadership is not simply a Catholic belief—it is the central line that was crossed when Luther and others rejected the pope's right to shepherd, teach, and correct in the name of Christ.

A Question of Authority: Who Decides?

The tragedy of the Reformation is not simply that it fractured visible unity—it redefined the very nature of truth in the Christian life. Without a universally recognized teaching authority, each believer was now left to decide for themselves what Scripture meant, how doctrine should develop, and what was essential to salvation.

Of course, few Protestants would claim they are the final authority. Most would say, "The Bible alone is my authority."

But here's the reality: Is it really the Bible that serves as the final arbiter... or is it their personal interpretation of the Bible?

This distinction is crucial.

Because two people can read the same verse and arrive at opposite conclusions. Ten people can form ten churches from the same chapter. And all of them can claim to be led by the Holy Spirit—while denying the guidance of the Church Christ founded and promised to lead into all truth (cf. John 16:13).

Chapter 14 will examine this foundational issue: Sola Scriptura—the idea that Scripture alone is sufficient for all matters of faith. We'll ask: Was this the belief of the early Church? Did the apostles teach it? And can it truly preserve unity in the Body of Christ?

Let's now explore where this doctrine came from, what it claims, and why—without the living voice of the Church—it ultimately cannot hold the Church together.

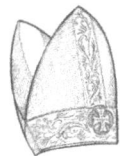  

Chapter 14

D.I.Y. Christianity

When Martin Luther broke from the Catholic Church, he may have believed that returning to "Scripture alone" would bring clarity to a Church he felt was losing its spiritual footing. But what followed was not the restoration of unity, nor the purification of the Church through debate and discernment. What followed was a shattering.

Christ prayed, "That they may all be one... so that the world may believe that you sent me" (John 17:21). But today, there are tens of thousands of Christian denominations, each with their own interpretations, traditions, and theologies. The Christian world has become a kaleidoscope of contradiction — vibrant, yes — but fractured.

And the root of that fracture can be traced to two rallying cries of the Protestant Reformation:

• Sola Scriptura – "Scripture alone"

• Sola Fide – "Faith alone"

Both sound noble on the surface, but neither hold together when examined in the light of Scripture, history, or logic.

Sola Scriptura: Whose Scripture? Whose Interpretation?

Sola Scriptura proclaims that the Bible alone is the final authority for faith and morals. But this principle immediately raises a critical question: Whose interpretation of the Bible?

Even among sincere and devout Christians, interpretations vary drastically:

• Baptists say baptism is symbolic.

• Lutherans say Christ is present in the Eucharist, but not literally.

• Methodists affirm female clergy.

• Pentecostals may reject sacraments altogether.

• Seventh-Day Adventists uphold Saturday worship based on the Jewish Sabbath.

They all appeal to Scripture — but arrive at vastly different conclusions. The Reformers rejected the Magisterium of the Catholic Church, but they did not erase the need for authority. They only replaced one teacher with thousands.

In effect, Sola Scriptura has led to Solo Scriptura — where every man becomes his own pope, deciding what the Bible "really says" based on his reading, his conscience, or his cultural context.

Even Martin Luther, in frustration with other Reformers, once exclaimed:

"There are as many sects and beliefs as there are heads."

He saw the fragmentation even in his own lifetime.

Sola Fide: Faith Without Form?

Likewise, the doctrine of "faith alone" — while intended to safeguard the primacy of grace — has often reduced Christianity to a personal feeling rather than a lived relationship within the Body of Christ.

James, in his epistle, directly challenges this idea:

"You see that a man is justified by works and not by faith alone" (James 2:24).

This verse is the only place in all of Scripture where the phrase "faith alone" appears — and it is explicitly rejected.

Salvation is not earned by works — Catholics agree wholeheartedly on that point. But neither is it a mere moment of mental agreement with Jesus. It is a lifelong journey of faith expressed in love (cf. Galatians 5:6). The sacraments are not optional spiritual accessories. They are the ordinary means Christ gave us for grace — real encounters, not empty symbols.

The Fruit of Fragmentation

Once these pillars took hold, division became a feature, not a bug, of Protestantism.

Without a central, divinely instituted authority to arbitrate theological disputes, new denominations emerged with alarming speed:

- Presbyterians from Calvinist roots

- Anabaptists who rejected infant baptism

- Quakers who rejected formal worship and clergy

- Pentecostals who emphasized charismatic gifts

- Evangelicals who emphasized a personal relationship with Jesus, often at the expense of sacramental theology

And from there, the spectrum only widened:

- Churches affirming same-sex marriage and those declaring it sinful

- Congregations ordaining women and others calling it unbiblical

- Denominations declaring each other's baptisms invalid

The Church that Christ founded — One, Holy, Catholic, and Apostolic — has been replaced in the minds of many by a sort of cafeteria of preferences.

Everyone a Pope

When someone no longer agrees with their pastor, they simply change churches. If they don't agree with their denomination, they start a new one. If they prefer livestream worship from the couch, they make "YouTube Church" their spiritual home. There is no hierarchy, no sacraments, no accountability — just personal conviction.

They may say that the Bible alone is their authority.

But in practice, it's not the Bible that acts as their arbiter.

It's their interpretation of the Bible — or that of their favorite speaker, teacher, or YouTube channel.

Setting the Stage for More Confusion

This chapter sets the stage for what comes next:

- What happens when the core truths of Christianity themselves are denied?

- What about groups like Jehovah's Witnesses, Mormons, and others who claim to be Christian — but reject Christ's divinity, the Trinity, or even the reality of the soul?

In the next chapter, we will meet some of the most *friendly*, *committed*, and *morally upright* people you'll ever encounter — and see how they've built entire systems on a foundation that is *anything but Christian*.

Chapter 15

Beware of Wolves in Sheeps Clothing

It's a tragic reality that some of the kindest, most dedicated, family-oriented people you'll meet belong to groups that claim to follow Christ—but actually promote teachings that completely dismantle the Christian Gospel.

Sincerity, after all, is not the same as truth.

Jehovah's Witnesses: A Gospel Without the Cross

Founded: By Charles Taze Russell in the 1870s, in Pennsylvania, USA.

Russell rejected many core Christian doctrines—including the Trinity, hell, and the eternal soul. He believed the Church had become corrupted early on and that his movement, originally called the "Bible Student movement," was a restoration of true Christianity.

Key Theological Errors:

• Jesus is not eternal God, but a created being—specifically, Michael the Archangel.

- The Trinity is denied as a pagan invention.

- The Cross is rejected as a symbol (Witnesses use a single-pole "stake" instead).

- Jesus did not rise bodily, but was recreated as a spirit-being after death.

- Only 144,000 will go to heaven; the rest of the faithful will live eternally on a renewed Earth.

These teachings echo Arianism, condemned at the Council of Nicaea in 325. The idea that Jesus is a creature and not consubstantial with the Father directly contradicts the core of the Christian faith.

And it gets more dangerous: the Jehovah's Witnesses discourage any independent reading of Scripture without Watchtower interpretation, and have retranslated the Bible (in the "New World Translation") to fit their doctrines—including modifying John 1:1 to say, *"the Word was a god."*

This is not biblical. This is not Christian. This is heresy in a necktie.

The Church of Jesus Christ of Latter-day Saints (Mormonism): The Divine Man and the Exalted Self

Founded: By Joseph Smith in 1830, in New York, USA.

Joseph Smith claimed to receive golden plates from the angel Moroni, which he translated into the Book of Mormon, a text he asserted was a fuller revelation of Jesus Christ in the Americas.

Key Theological Errors:

- God the Father has a physical body, was once a man, and became a god.

- Jesus is the spirit-brother of Lucifer, not the eternal Son consubstantial with the Father.

- Faithful Mormons can become gods themselves—a belief known as *exaltation* or *eternal progression*.

- The Bible is respected "as far as it is translated correctly," but subordinated to the Book of Mormon, the Doctrine and Covenants, and the Pearl of Great Price.

- Salvation is works-based and requires temple rites, secret rituals, and eternal marriage.

This is not Christianity in any historic or orthodox sense. It is polytheism in disguise, wrapped in family values and missionary smiles. The Mormon Jesus is not the Jesus of the Nicene Creed, nor of the Gospels. He is not co-eternal, not fully divine, and not the second Person of the Trinity as Christianity has always professed.

Smith's revelations created an entirely different religion, though one that often borrows Christian language and values to appear familiar.

Christian Science: Denying the Material and the Incarnate

Founded: By Mary Baker Eddy in 1879, in Massachusetts, USA.

After a personal healing experience, Eddy wrote *Science and Health with Key to the Scriptures*, asserting that all matter—including sickness, sin, and even death—is an illusion, and that true spiritual understanding leads to healing.

Key Theological Errors:

- Jesus is not God but a divine *idea*.

- There is no physical resurrection, no literal sin, and no need for the Cross.

- The material world is unreal; pain and disease are errors of the mind.

- Salvation is not through grace, but through right thinking.

While promoting peace and healing, Christian Science undermines the entire Christian narrative—denying the Incarnation, the Passion, and the bodily Resurrection of Christ. Its metaphysics overlap with Gnosticism, which the early Church rejected for denying the goodness of the physical world and Christ's real humanity.

A Shared Pattern: When Christ Is Reimagined, Christianity Collapses

What do all of these groups have in common?

1 A charismatic founder claiming *special revelation*.

2 A rejection of historic Christian doctrine, especially about Christ's nature.

3 A new scripture or reinterpretation of the Bible.

4 A dismissal of Church authority, often replacing it with an authoritarian internal hierarchy.

5 And a subtle but absolute claim: *"Everyone else is wrong. Only we have the truth."*

But if Christ is not fully God, if the Cross is just symbolic, and if salvation depends on secret knowledge or personal merit, then we are no longer in the realm of Christianity. We're back in the ancient heresies that the Church has already named and answered.

The kindness of their members should never mask the reality that these belief systems lead people away from the living Christ, and away from the Church He founded.

More Than Just Good Intentions

As we reflect on the dizzying variety of religious movements that have sprung up over the last few centuries—Jehovah's Witnesses, Mormons, Christian Scientists, and others—we must ask: *Do these teachings resemble what we find in the Gospels? Do they echo the voice of Christ or the structure of His Church as it took form in the Acts of the Apostles?*

Look closely at the New Testament. What do we find?

We see Peter, personally commissioned by Christ, boldly leading the Church (cf. Matthew 16:18–19; Acts 2). We see apostolic authority established, defended, and passed on. We see bishops, elders, and deacons appointed—not self-proclaimed prophets writing new books of Scripture. We see unity maintained through shared belief, sacramental life, and communion with the visible Church—not fragmentation and theological innovation.

Where are the Mormons or Jehovah's Witnesses calling for unity with the Orthodox? Where is their recognition of the bishop of Rome as a successor of Peter? Where is their continuity with the saints, martyrs, and councils of the early Church?

It isn't there.

And that's the point.

The chaos is not merely unfortunate—it's a rupture. A tearing away from the fabric of the faith once delivered to the saints (cf. Jude 1:3). These groups, however sincere their members may be, promote doctrines so incompatible with historic Christianity that even the earliest Christians would hardly recognize them as belonging to the same faith.

This is not just about preference, personality, or style. It's about truth.

And truth doesn't evolve into contradiction.

The Lord promised to send the Spirit of Truth to guide His Church (cf. John 16:13). He didn't say He would guide *everyone individually into their own version* of the truth. He established a Church—visible, sacramental, apostolic, and united—not a scattering of good ideas with no tether to what He actually taught.

And so we end this chapter with a stark but necessary observation:

If what you believe bears no resemblance to the Christianity taught, lived, and safeguarded by the early Church, then it is not the fullness of the faith Christ gave the world.

It may be passionate. It may be well-intentioned. But it is not the Church He founded.

And truth, if it is truly truth, must be whole.

Chapter 16

The Biblical Blueprint of the Catholic Church

The Blueprint, Written in Red

It began not with a scroll, but with a question.

"Who do you say that I am?" (Matthew 16:15)

Jesus asked it not to the crowds, but to His closest followers. And in a moment of Spirit-filled clarity, Simon answered—not as a fisherman, but as a man being called out of his old life into something eternal:

"You are the Christ, the Son of the living God."

"Blessed are you, Simon son of Jonah... You are Peter, and on this rock I will build my Church."

In just a few lines of Scripture, something extraordinary happened: Jesus didn't simply affirm Peter's answer. He *established* something new—His Church. Not a metaphor. Not a vague community of like-minded believers. But a living, breathing structure entrusted to human hands and divine grace. And Peter, the imperfect, impulsive man, became the rock beneath it.

This wasn't a reward. It was a mission.

Jesus didn't need to use the language of building and binding. He didn't have to mention keys. But He did. Because this Church would not survive on inspiration alone. It needed foundation. It needed leadership. It needed continuity.

Just as David's kingdom had a chief steward (cf. Isaiah 22), the Kingdom of God would have a visible representative—one who held the keys, not for personal power, but for the sake of unity and order. This is the Biblical blueprint: a visible Church, guided by spiritual fathers, formed through sacraments, and sent into the world to proclaim, teach, forgive, and heal.

It's no accident that in the Book of Acts, Peter speaks first, acts first, decides first. It's no surprise that when controversy arises, the Church doesn't split. Instead, the apostles meet in council (Acts 15), discern together, and speak with one voice: *"It has seemed good to the Holy Spirit and to us…"*

What we see in the New Testament is a Church that is both human and divine—fragile in its members, firm in its foundation. It doesn't always move quickly. It doesn't always look glorious. But it stands.

The blueprint is not democratic. It's sacramental.

It doesn't invite everyone to write their own version of truth. It invites everyone to be drawn into *the* truth—through baptism, the Eucharist, the laying on of hands, and the Word proclaimed and guarded by those sent to do so.

The apostles knew their mission would outlive them. That's why they chose successors. That's why Paul urged Timothy to appoint trustworthy men to teach others (2 Timothy 2:2). The Church was never meant to rely on personal charisma or individual interpretation. It was built to last, through the storm and the centuries.

And so it has.

The blueprint drawn by Christ—sketched in parables, etched in blood, and handed to trembling hands—continues. Not as a relic, but as a reality.

We are not left to wander. The Church Christ built on a sure foundation remains guided by Truth.

The Rock Still Stands

Peter's story is not merely woven into the New Testament—it dominates its narrative.

From the Gospels to the early Church in Acts, Peter's name surfaces more than any other apostle. While all the apostles are important, Peter is mentioned by name 191 times (as *Simon*, *Peter*, or *Simon Peter*)—far more than any other.

For comparison:

- Peter – 191 times
- John – ~48 times
- James (the Greater) – ~18 times
- Andrew – ~13 times
- All other apostles combined – ~130 times

The numbers alone tell part of the story. But what makes this even more remarkable is what Peter is doing in those moments:

Unique Roles & Decisions Assigned to Peter

1 Name Change & Foundation of the Church

  ◦ *"You are Peter (Kepha), and on this rock I will build my Church..."* (Matthew 16:18)

- Only Simon receives a name change from Jesus—signaling a change in identity and mission.

2 Given the Keys to the Kingdom

- *"I will give you the keys of the kingdom of heaven..."* (Matthew 16:19)

- Echoes Isaiah 22:22, where keys represent delegated royal authority.

3 Entrusted to Strengthen the Brethren

- *"I have prayed for you, Simon, that your faith may not fail. And when you have turned back, strengthen your brothers."* (Luke 22:32)

4 Given the Shepherding Role

- After the Resurrection, Jesus reinstates Peter with a triple command: *"Feed my lambs... Tend my sheep... Feed my sheep."* (John 21:15–17)

5 Spokesman for the Apostles

- He frequently speaks on behalf of the Twelve (e.g., Matthew 16:16; John 6:68–69; Acts 2:14).

6 Performs the First Apostolic Miracle

- He heals a lame beggar at the Temple gate. (Acts 3:1–10)

7 Delivers the First Apostolic Sermon

- At Pentecost, Peter explains the descent of the Holy Spirit and calls for repentance. (Acts 2:14–41)

8 Decides Church Discipline

- Condemns Ananias and Sapphira for lying to the Holy Spirit. (Acts 5:1–11)

9 Welcomes the First Gentile Converts

- Baptizes Cornelius and his household after receiving a vision from God. (Acts 10–11)

10 Presides at the First Church Council

- At the Council of Jerusalem, Peter stands and speaks with finality about the Gentile question. (Acts 15:7–11)

11 Rebukes Heresy & False Worship

- Confronts Simon the Magician. (Acts 8:20–23)

12 Miraculously Delivered from Prison

- An angel frees him from chains, underscoring his role and God's protection. (Acts 12)

13 Recognized as "First" Among the Apostles

- *"The names of the twelve apostles are these: first, Simon who is called Peter..."* (Matthew 10:2)

- The Greek word πρῶτος (*prōtos*) indicates primacy—not chronology, but rank.

Peter is not flawless. He stumbles. He denies Jesus. But he weeps and returns. And it is Peter—*not John, not James*—who is asked to shepherd the flock.

The pattern is clear: whenever a key moment of decision, leadership, or transition emerges, Peter is either central or singular in his role.

Even Paul, known for confronting Peter in Galatians 2 over behavior —not doctrine—still sought Peter's approval for his Gospel mission (cf. Galatians 1:18; 2:1–2). That visit to Jerusalem was not casual. Paul spent 15 days with Peter, not just to chat—but to confirm the unity of faith and mission.

Where is Peter Now?

The legacy of Peter did not end with his martyrdom in Rome. That same city still holds the relics of his bones beneath the altar of St. Peter's Basilica, and his office continues through apostolic succession in the bishop of Rome.

The rock still stands—not because Peter was perfect, but because Christ is.

Not because men are always faithful, but because God is.

The blueprint was not just drawn. It was built. And it still shelters those who wish to remain in communion with the One Shepherd.

The Cost of Disconnection

When Jesus established His Church, He gave it form, function, and foundation. He did not intend for it to fracture. His prayer in John 17 was that His followers might be one—united in truth, love, and mission. And yet, as history marched forward, division crept in.

The cost of this disconnection has been staggering.

Without a central shepherd, tens of thousands of separate communities now interpret Scripture on their own terms. One pastor proclaims baptism as necessary, another says it's optional. One group believes the Eucharist is truly Christ; another dismisses it as a mere symbol. Moral teachings shift with culture, not with Christ. The same Bible is held up, but its meaning fractures like a shattered mirror—each shard reflecting a piece, none reflecting the whole.

This was never God's design.

Saint Paul warned of this in his letters—urging believers not to say, "I follow Paul" or "I follow Apollos" (cf. 1 Corinthians 1:12), but to remain united in Christ, under the guidance of those entrusted to lead in fidelity to the Gospel. The New Testament does not envision a loose network of believers all arriving at their own conclusions. It shows a Church with real decisions, real discipline, real sacraments, and real authority.

The disconnection from Peter's successors is not just administrative—it is spiritual.

As Saint Cyprian of Carthage famously warned in the third century: *"He who does not have the Church as his mother cannot have God as his Father."* That may sound harsh to modern ears, but his point was not elitism—it was about truth. There is one Church established by Christ, one Eucharist, one baptism, one faith (cf. Ephesians 4:4–5). To walk away from the Body is to risk walking away from the fullness of Christ.

Even among Christian groups that strive to be faithful, the absence of a final authority has led to increasing confusion and contradiction. Everyone becomes a pope unto themselves. But Christ did not build His Church on everyone. He built it on Peter. The Church is not a theological democracy. It is a divine institution, safeguarded by the Holy Spirit and guided by a living voice.

Disconnection always brings a cost. And yet, Christ's call to unity is not canceled by human failure. The gate is still open. The Church still stands. And the Rock still holds.

A Church Both Visible and Victorious

The Catholic Church is not a denomination. We never broke off. We didn't "denominate" from anyone. We are not one among many. We are the Church Christ Himself founded—wounded at times, misunderstood often, and yet still standing. Still home.

Ours is a history both glorious and torn. There have been golden ages of faith and beauty, and centuries of scandal and division. And yet… we are still here. Not because of our merit, but because of Christ's mercy. Not because we have done all things well, but because He has never abandoned His Bride.

We look across the Tiber with deep longing toward our Orthodox brothers and sisters—not in triumphalism, but in love. We cheer them on. We honor their faith. We mourn the schism, but we also rejoice in what still unites us: valid sacraments, apostolic succession, deep reverence for mystery and liturgy. And we pray for the day when full communion is restored—not through compromise, but through clarity and charity.

We fight—yes, fight—for our Protestant brothers and sisters as well. Not with hostility, but with hope. We see their love for Scripture. We honor their desire for personal relationship with Christ. We grieve the misunderstandings and centuries of division. But we will never stop welcoming them home—not to a better place, but to the fullness of what Christ gave: a Church that is sacramental, apostolic, Eucharistic, and one.

Peter is still here. Not because he is better than the others, but because Christ chose him to be a visible sign of unity.

Not every Catholic lives this mission well. Many don't. But the Church does. The Church endures. The Church keeps calling her children home, one by one, with the same arms that welcomed them at the font of baptism and long to nourish them at the altar.

This is not a battle cry for winners. This is a cry of the Bride for her family to be reunited.

There is only one Church Jesus built.

It's not ours. It's His.

And He entrusted it to Peter, not as a private throne, but as a public signpost—pointing always to Christ, the Cornerstone, the Savior, the Shepherd.

We are not perfect.

But we are home.

And we are waiting.

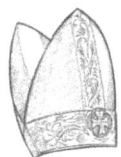  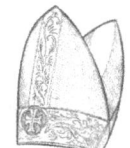

Chapter 17

Conclusion

That They May Be One

There is something profoundly human—and profoundly divine—about longing for home.

From the earliest moments of Christianity, the Church was never meant to be a fractured collection of well-meaning communities. She was always meant to be a family, united in faith, rooted in the teachings of the apostles, and bound together in the love of Christ. Her authority was not established to dominate, but to protect. Her liturgy was not composed to impress, but to elevate. Her sacraments were not invented, but entrusted—by Christ Himself—to be the ordinary means of grace for the salvation of the world.

And yet, here we are, over two thousand years later, surrounded by division, debate, and disconnection.

Some see this and walk away. Others decide it doesn't matter. Still others choose to cling to their version of Christianity, even if it no longer resembles anything found in the New Testament.

But there are also those who pause, who pray, who search for the Church that Jesus Himself founded—not just an idea or an echo of that Church, but the actual, visible, historical, living Body of Christ on earth.

That Church is the Catholic Church.

She did not denominate from anything. She did not come later. She was born at Pentecost, built upon the rock of Peter, sustained by the apostles and their successors, and preserved by the Holy Spirit even when battered by scandal, sin, and suffering. Her scars are real. But so is her foundation. And it is unshakable.

She is not perfect because of her members, but because of her Master.

She is not strong because of her leaders, but because of her Lord.

She is not enduring because of strategy or adaptation, but because of a promise:

> "You are Peter, and on this rock I will build my Church, and the gates of hell shall not prevail against it." (Mt 16:18)

We live in an age where everyone is encouraged to follow their own truth. But truth cannot contradict itself. If Jesus Christ is the same yesterday, today, and forever (cf. Heb 13:8), then so must be His Church. The same Church that confirmed the canon of Scripture is the one that faithfully teaches how to interpret it. The same Church that has faced emperors, heresies, wars, and reformations still stands —beaten, bruised, misunderstood, and even hated—but still speaking with the same voice, offering the same grace, and proclaiming the same Christ.

This is not a call to triumphalism. It is a call to humility.

To ask: *What if the Church I've rejected was never what I thought it was?*

To wonder: *What if Christ really did establish something visible?*

To consider: *What if God is calling me home—not just to an idea of Christianity, but to its fullness?*

The Catholic Church does not rejoice in division. She grieves it. But she also continues to extend her arms, to welcome, to teach, and to invite. She is not merely preserving tradition; she is proclaiming Christ, crucified and risen, in every age and every culture.

We long for unity because we were made for communion. And while theological dialogues and ecumenical efforts continue, so does the voice of Peter—echoing through history, through the noise, through the hurt:

"Lord, to whom shall we go? You have the words of eternal life." (Jn 6:68)

Let us go to Him together. Let us pray for one another. And let us walk forward—not in suspicion or pride, but in hope. Because the Shepherd still calls. The Church still stands. And the door is still open.

Ut unum sint. That they may be one.

Prayer for Christian Unity

Eternal Father,

You sent Your Son to gather what was scattered,

To heal what was broken,

To restore what was lost.

Look with mercy upon Your Church,

Torn by division and wounded by pride.

We confess the sins of our past,

The failures of our witness,

And the scandal of our disunity.

Lord Jesus,

You prayed that we might be one,

Even as You and the Father are one.

Let not Your prayer go unanswered in our time.

Soften hardened hearts,

Mend what has been shattered,

And bring Your children home.

Holy Spirit,

You are the bond of love between the Father and the Son.

Be the bond of peace among all who bear the name Christian.

Illuminate our minds,

Purify our motives,

And guide us into all truth.

Help us to see one another not as enemies or strangers,

But as brothers and sisters called to the same table,

Longing for the same Lord,

And redeemed by the same blood.

We ask this through the intercession of the Blessed Virgin Mary,

Mother of the Church,

And through all the saints who prayed, served, and suffered for the unity of Your people.

Amen.

Bibliography

The following resources contributed to the contents in this book.

Akin, Jimmy. *The Fathers Know Best: Your Essential Guide to the Teachings of the Early Church*. Catholic Answers, 2010.
Athanasius of Alexandria. *Four Discourses Against the Arians*. Translated by John Henry Newman and Archibald Robertson. *Nicene and Post-Nicene Fathers*, Series II, Vol. 4. Christian Literature Publishing Co., 1892.
Barron, Robert. *Catholicism: A Journey to the Heart of the Faith*. New York: Image Books, 2011.
Benedict XVI (Joseph Ratzinger). *Called to Communion: Understanding the Church Today*. San Francisco: Ignatius Press, 1996.
Bokenkotter, Thomas. *A Concise History of the Catholic Church*. Image Books, 2004.
Bordeianu, Radu. *Eastern Catholic Churches: Identity, Ecclesiology, and Renewal*. University of Notre Dame Press, 2014.
Bowman, Robert M. Jr., and J. Ed Komoszewski. *Putting Jesus in His Place: The Case for the Deity of Christ*. Kregel Publications, 2007.
Brown, Raymond E. *An Introduction to the New Testament*. Yale University Press, 1997.
Bruce, F. F. *Peter: The Prince of Apostles*. Grand Rapids: Eerdmans, 1958.
Butler, Alban. *Lives of the Saints* (entry on St. Peter), various editions.
Carson, D. A. *Expositor's Bible Commentary: Matthew*. Edited by Frank E. Gaebelein. Grand Rapids: Zondervan, 1984.
Catechism of the Catholic Church. 2nd ed. Vatican City: Libreria Editrice Vaticana, 1997.
Chadwick, Henry. *East and West: The Making of a Rift in the Church: From Apostolic Times until the Council of Florence*. Oxford University Press, 2003.
Chadwick, Henry. *The Early Church*. Revised Edition. Penguin Books, 1993.
Chrysostom, John. *Homilies on the Gospel of John*. Nicene and Post-Nicene Fathers, First Series, Vol. 14. Christian Literature Publishing Co., 1889.
Chrysostom, John. *Homilies on the Gospel of Matthew*. Nicene and Post-Nicene Fathers, First Series, Vol. 10. Christian Literature Publishing Co., 1888.
Code of Canons of the Eastern Churches. Vatican City: Libreria Editrice Vaticana, 1990.
Congregation for the Eastern Churches. *Instruction for Applying the Liturgical Prescriptions of the Code of Canons of the Eastern Churches*, 1996.
Cross, F. L., and E. A. Livingstone, editors. *The Oxford Dictionary of the Christian Church*. 3rd ed., Oxford University Press, 2005.
Cullmann, Oscar. *Peter: Disciple, Apostle, Martyr*. Translated by Floyd V. Filson. Philadelphia: Westminster Press, 1953.

Denzinger, Heinrich. *The Sources of Catholic Dogma.* Translated by Roy J. Deferrari. Loreto Publications, 1957.

Duffy, Eamon. *Saints and Sinners: A History of the Popes.* Yale University Press, 2006.

Dvornik, Francis. *The Photian Schism: History and Legend.* Cambridge University Press, 1948.

Eddy, Mary Baker. *Science and Health with Key to the Scriptures.* Boston: The First Church of Christ, Scientist, 1875.

Eusebius of Caesarea. *Ecclesiastical History.* c. A.D. 325.

Eusebius of Caesarea. *The Church History.* Translated by Paul L. Maier. Grand Rapids, MI: Kregel Publications, 1999.

FairMormon Staff. "Does the LDS Church Believe God Was Once a Man?" FAIR Latter-day Saints.

Florovsky, Georges. *The Catholicity of the Church.* Geneva: WCC Publications, 1934. Reprinted in *Bible, Church, Tradition.* Belmont, MA: Nordland, 1972.

Fortescue, Adrian. *The Orthodox Eastern Church.* Catholic Way Publishing, 2014.

France, R.T. *The Gospel of Matthew.* Grand Rapids: Eerdmans, 2007.

Gallaro, Kurt Burnette. "Eastern Catholic Churches in Full Communion with the Holy See." *Eastern Catholic Life,* 2020.

Geisler, Norman L., and Ron Rhodes. *Correcting the Cults.* Baker Books, 2005.

González, Justo L. *The Story of Christianity: Volume 1.* HarperOne, 2010.

Hahn, Scott. *A Father Who Keeps His Promises.* Cincinnati: St. Anthony Messenger Press, 1998.

Hahn, Scott. *Many Are Called.* New York: Doubleday, 2010.

Hahn, Scott. *Upon This Rock.* New York: Image Books, 1999.

Hall, Stuart G. *Doctrine and Practice in the Early Church.* Wipf & Stock Publishers, 1992.

Ignatius of Antioch. *Letter to the Smyrnaeans and Letter to the Romans.* In *The Apostolic Fathers,* Harvard University Press, 2003.

Ignatius of Antioch. *Letters.* c. A.D. 107.

Irenaeus. *Against Heresies.* In *The Ante-Nicene Fathers,* Vol. 1. Eerdmans, 1885.

John Paul II. *Ut Unum Sint.* Vatican City: Libreria Editrice Vaticana, 1995.

Kelly, J. N. D. *Early Christian Doctrines.* 5th ed. San Francisco: HarperOne, 2004.

Kreeft, Peter. *Catholic Christianity.* San Francisco: Ignatius Press, 2001.

Lawler, Ronald. *The Teaching of Christ.* Huntington, IN: Our Sunday Visitor, 2000.

Leo I (Pope). *Tome of Leo.* In *Nicene and Post-Nicene Fathers,* Series II, Vol. 12. Christian Literature Publishing Co., 1895.

Leo XIII. *Orientalium Dignitas.* Apostolic Letter, 1894.

Luther, Martin. *Table Talk.* London: George Bell & Sons, 1901.

Luther, Martin. *The Babylonian Captivity of the Church.* 1520.

Martin, Walter. *The Kingdom of the Cults.* Bethany House, 2003.

Mathison, Keith A. *The Shape of Sola Scriptura.* Canon Press, 2001.

McGrath, Alister. *Christian Theology: An Introduction.* Wiley-Blackwell, 2016.

Meyendorff, John. *Byzantine Theology.* Fordham University Press, 1983.

Bibliography

Mitch, Curtis, and Edward Sri. *The Gospel of Matthew.* Baker Academic, 2010.

New World Translation of the Holy Scriptures. Watch Tower Bible and Tract Society of Pennsylvania, 2013.

Newman, John Henry. *An Essay on the Development of Christian Doctrine.* University of Notre Dame Press, 1989.

Pelikan, Jaroslav. *The Christian Tradition, Vol. 1.* University of Chicago Press, 1971.

Pelikan, Jaroslav. *The Riddle of Roman Catholicism.* New York: Abingdon Press, 1959.

Pontifical Council for Promoting Christian Unity. *The Catholic Church and the Orthodox Church: A Common Road to Unity.* Vatican Publishing, 2000.

Ray, Stephen K. *Upon This Rock.* San Francisco: Ignatius Press, 1999.

Rhodes, Ron. *The Challenge of the Cults and New Religions.* Zondervan, 2001.

Runciman, Steven. *The Eastern Schism.* Oxford University Press, 1955.

Ratzinger, Joseph. *Called to Communion.* San Francisco: Ignatius Press, 1996.

RSVCE – Revised Standard Version, Catholic Edition. Scripture translation used throughout.

Schaff, Philip, and Henry Wace, editors. *Nicene and Post-Nicene Fathers,* Series II. Christian Literature Publishing Co., 1890–1900.

Schreck, Alan. *Catholic and Christian.* Servant Books, 2004.

Shelley, Bruce L. *Church History in Plain Language.* 4th ed., Thomas Nelson, 2013.

Shevchuk, Sviatoslav. "On the Relationship Between the Ukrainian Greek Catholic Church and the Orthodox Churches." *Ukrainian Catholic University Publications,* 2022.

Smith, Joseph. *The Book of Mormon.* Salt Lake City: The Church of Jesus Christ of Latter-day Saints, 1830.

St. Clement of Rome. *Letter to the Corinthians,* c. A.D. 96.

St. Gregory the Great. *Letters and Homilies.* Papacy 590–604.

St. Maximus the Confessor. d. A.D. 662.

Strong, James. *Strong's Exhaustive Concordance of the Bible.* Nashville: Abingdon Press, 1890.

Thomas Aquinas, St. *Summa Theologiae, Supplementum.* London: Burns, Oates & Washbourne, 1920.

Thomas, Yannick. "The Papacy and the Eastern Churches in the First Millennium." *Catholic Answers,* 2020.

Trent, Council of. *Decree Concerning Justification,* Session VI, 1547.

United States Conference of Catholic Bishops. *Catholic Answers on Cults and New Religious Movements.*

Vatican Council II. *Orientalium Ecclesiarum (Decree on the Catholic Churches of the Eastern Rite),* 1964.

Ware, Kallistos. *The Orthodox Church.* Penguin Books, 1993.

Watchtower Bible and Tract Society. *What Does the Bible Really Teach?* Brooklyn, NY: Watch Tower Bible and Tract Society, 2005.

White, James R. *The Forgotten Trinity.* Bethany House, 1998.

White, James R. *The Roman Catholic Controversy.* Bethany House Publishers, 1996.

Wilken, Robert Louis. *The Spirit of Early Christian Thought: Seeking the Face of God.* Yale University Press, 2003.

Wuellner, Wilhelm H. *The Meaning of 'Episkopos' in Early Christian Literature.* London: SPCK, 1954.

Zizoulas, John D. *Being as Communion: Studies in Personhood and the Church.* St. Vladimir's Seminary Press, 1985.

About the Author

John Henry is a Catholic writer, educator, leadership coach, and the founder of *Always Toward the Light*—a faith-based publication dedicated to truth, unity, and spiritual renewal. A former school principal, firefighter, and professional horse trainer, his life has been marked by both great heights and profound challenges. These experiences have deepened his love for Christ and his passion for the Church He founded.

John's journey into Catholic apologetics emerged from a lifelong hunger for truth and a desire to help others rediscover the beauty, clarity, and authority of the Catholic faith. He is the author of *The Skeptical Catholic*, a published work that engages seekers, skeptics, and cradle Catholics with honest answers to hard questions. He is also the creator of the beloved *Little Letters from Jesus* series, a collection of intimate spiritual reflections written in the voice of Christ, offering readers comfort, challenge, and hope.

With a heart for unity and a fire for clarity, John writes to reach Catholics who have grown disillusioned, Protestants who are seeking more, and anyone who dares to believe that the gates of hell will not prevail.

He lives by the words: *"One step at a time, always toward the Light."*

You can read more from John or connect with him at www.AlwaysTowardTheLight.org.

▶ youtube.com/@alwaystowardthelight
🦋 bsky.app/profile/faith-and-reason.bsky.social
𝕏 x.com/AlwaysToward

www.ingramcontent.com/pod-product-compliance
Lightning Source LLC
Chambersburg PA
CBHW070458100426
42743CB00010B/1678